ON
THE
ARTS

ON
THE
ARTS

ESSAYS BY
NAOMI BETH WAKAN

SHANTI ARTS PUBLISHING
BRUNSWICK MAINE

ON THE ARTS

Published by Shanti Arts Publishing

Cover and interior design by Shanti Arts Designs

Shanti Arts LLC
Brunswick, Maine
www.shantiarts.com

Printed in the United States of America

The following essays first appeared in *Still Point Arts Quarterly*: "The Art of Domesticity," "The Art of Happy Architecture," "The Art of Solitude," "Film Noir," "Some Thoughts on the Creative Process," and the following first appeared in *Stone Voices*: "Art in Confinement," "The Art of Ikebana," "The Art of Japanese Calligraphy."

Poems on pages 7, 41, and 118 are by Naomi Beth Wakan

ISBN: 978-1-951651-09-1 (softcover)
ISBN: 978-1-951651-10-7 (ebook)

Library of Congress Control Number: 2020930414

To Eli, for although he moves at a snail's pace, his slow but steady rhythm grounds my spasmodic exuberance into sensible proportions.

And to Phillip Lopate, my adopted father, for my personal essays; he has inspired so many writers and made the personal essay a welcome genre.

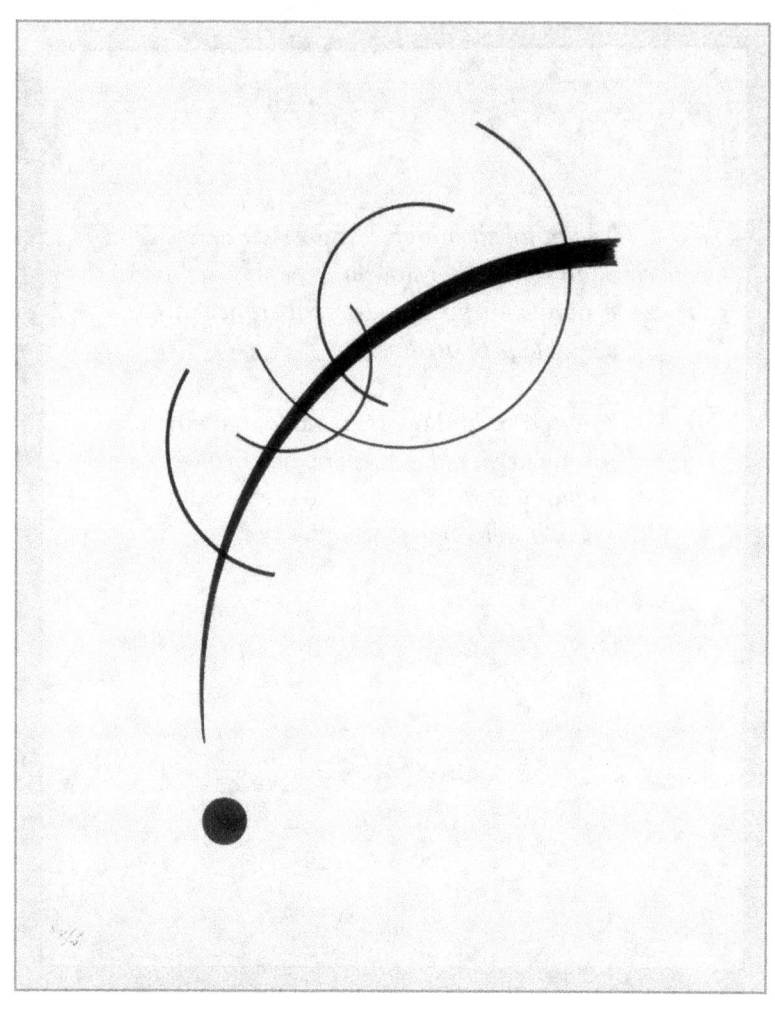

Wassily Kandinsky, *Free Curve to the Point - Accompanying
Sound of Geometric Curves*, 1925

The start of modern art

And Kandinsky came in
from the meadow one day
and, glancing at his easel,
shifted uneasily,
not quite knowing why.
It was at that moment
that modern art was born.
For on his canvas,
no meadows, no grasses
no bushes, no trees . . .
only colors and shapes
on his upside-down-placed canvas
and, if he had been
a flashy artist,
he would have jumped in the air
and turned somersaults.
But being severe and sober,
he merely coughed slightly
and smiled in a bemused way,
realizing that somehow he had
freed art from its subject,
by accident as it were;
shifted art toward music
by a mistake, and,
as he stared in wonder,
the bells rang out loud
from his canvas.

Contents

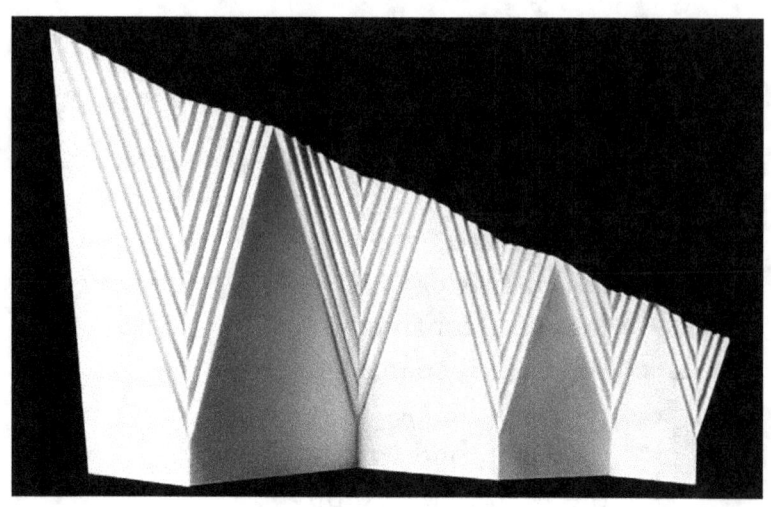

Elias Wakan, *Landscape 4*

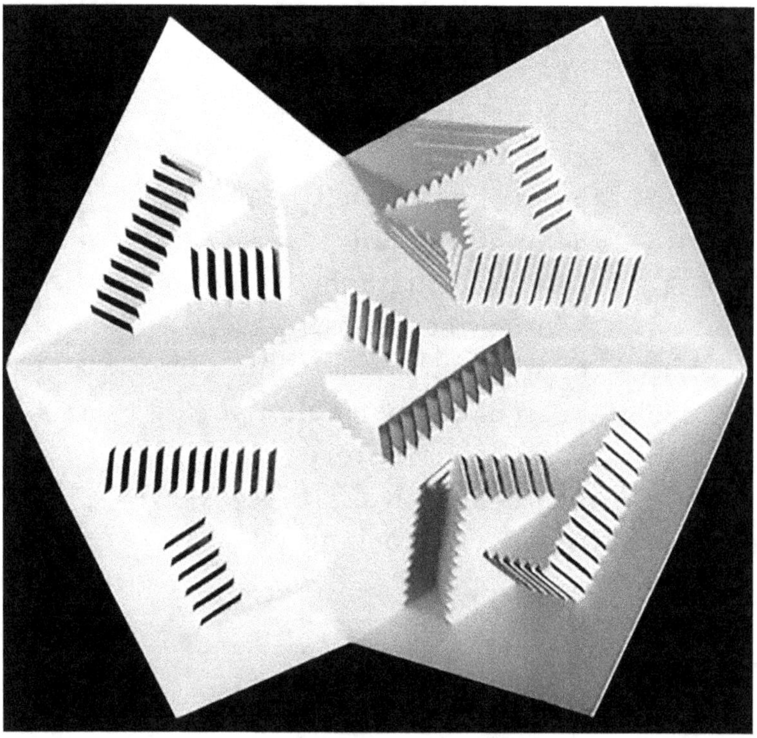

Elias Wakan, *Fold 4*

introduction

Every man is at liberty to understand nothing about anything.
  —Montaigne

IF HAVING TWICE BEEN MARRIED TO ARTISTS QUALIFIES
me for anything besides cleaning studios and helping with
promotion, it qualifies me to have a keen eye for art. With
my first husband, I frequented galleries in Toronto and
Buffalo, New York, and learned to "see" while acting as his
darkroom assistant. With my second husband, I became a
photographer myself and also tried my hand at painting and
fiber arts, as well as taking a closer look at sculptors, for he
is one. Thanks to both husbands—and a few other factors,
such as genes—I have a developed eye and a hand that has
held brushes, needles, and cameras. I have also written
promotional material, approached galleries and critics,
and mingled with wealthy collectors. It has not been an
unalloyed pleasurable journey, for the creating of art is one
thing, but its promotion and sale quite another. Even with
my own present creativity as a personal essayist and poet, I
have struggled with impasses, have longed for inspiration
when it didn't come, and have sometimes been overwhelmed
with its intensity when it did.

But the "fine arts," which is what I am speaking
of, are hardly relevant today. My 1960s-art-scene self
would hardly recognize the art scene today. The "art as
investment" crowd is still around, but art has jumped from

the galleries and museums to the streets and small stages. Art today is as diverse as graffiti, small embroidered pieces, and mimes. It has blended with craft and is, perhaps, reassuming its original meaning: any activity done with intensity that is the expression of human skill and imagination.

The personal essays in this collection were written so I might explore my own definition of "the arts." Among the wide range of subjects of these essays are many that have absorbed me at various times in my life. The ones resulting from my years of living in Japan include the arts of *ikebana* (flower arranging), *shodō* (calligraphy), and *haiga* (haiku linked to an image). I have also mused about what it must be like to create under confining conditions or if one has been marginalized. I have discussed my role models for my essay writing, spoken about the voices of singers, waxed poetic on a dance form I once studied, and as a rather domestic poet myself and one who considers cooking a fine art, I have included an essay on the art of food writing as well as one on domesticity as an art in itself. I've written on happy architecture and of my strange enchantment with the architect Gaudi, recalling that in my teenage years I had the desire that somewhere in my future there would be an architect. There wasn't, but I almost fulfilled my wish by building an earth-sheltered house with my present husband, Elias Wakan, who later developed into a constructivist sculptor, his creations being as close to miniature buildings as one would wish.

I am not an academic who researches a subject deeply, but a skimmer who scoops up the odd angle that attracts me, such as the glint of a piece of beach glass on a bed of seaweed. Sometimes, as I am an amateur in most arts, these cullings cast a strange light on accepted concepts—the naive telling of the Emperor's new clothes, as it were.

I trust that this collection of essays captures something of the peculiar creative world in which I have been willingly trapped in this lifetime. May the questions I have asked myself encourage you to ask questions too. Questions are good and often the spurs to inspiration. For example, consider the following from *For Adults Only*, by Beverly Nichols:

Child: "What are all these people looking at, Mummy?"
Mother: "It must be the picture of the year."
Child: "What is the picture of the year?"
Mother: "It is the picture that arouses the greatest interest."
Child: "Why? Because it is so beautiful?"
Mother: "Not exactly that."
Child: "Then why does it arouse so much interest?"
Mother: "Because nobody quite knows what it means."
Child: "Then why doesn't the artist tell them?"

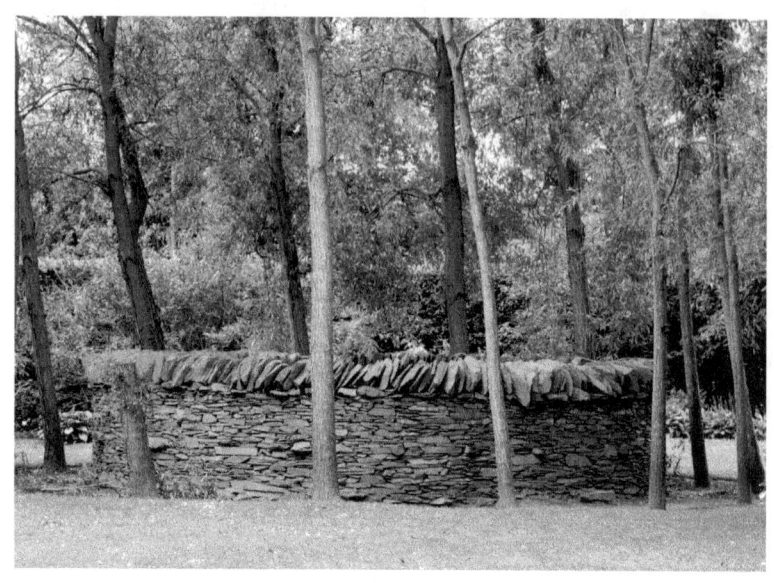

Sculpture by Andy Goldsworthy

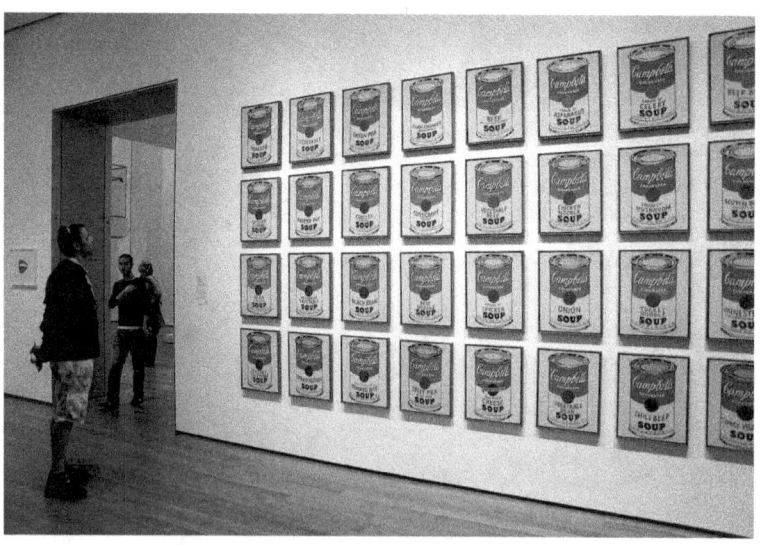

Andy Warhol's *Campbell Soup Cans*

what is art?

WHAT IS AN OLD-FASHIONED FUDDY-DUDDY LIKE ME TO do when confronted with a piece of art by Carl Andre, who assembled different arrangements of 120 fire bricks; by Douglas Gordon, who was paid for supplying a list of people he was remembering whose names then got placed on a gallery wall; by Damien Hirst, who created an exhibition of medicine cabinets filled with pills; by Jeff Koons, who exhibited a shampoo-polisher in vitrine; by Chris Ofili, whose painting of the Virgin Mary incorporated elephant dung; or by Felix Gonzales-Torres, who placed seven hundred pounds of wrapped liquorice and a pile of ten thousand fortune cookies on the floor. Are such objects really art? Part of my mind still equates art with fine art—things that hang in galleries, stand on public plinths, or hang over the couch. How antiquated can my idea be?

Just considering all the various fluctuations in what has been accepted as art in my lifetime has me bedazzled. Here are just a few:

Abstract Expressionism: action painting, color-field painting, exploration of form and color

Outsider Art: not really a movement but an acceptance of the art of "eccentric" people

Op Art: popularized by Victor Vasarely and Bridget Riley, this is art that has you blinking when you try to focus on it

Kinetic Art: popularized by Alexander Calder and Jean Tinguely, such art moves and sometimes blows itself up

Pop Art: examples are reproductions of Campbell's soup cans and multiple images of Marilyn Monroe

Minimalist Art: associated with Agnes Martin and other white-on-white and one color painters

Magical Realism: features everyday reality with an element of fantasy, associated with Paul Cadmus

Happenings: mixed-media events that challenge the audience

Video Art: shattered understandings of art as mainly painting, photography, and sculpture

Conceptual Art: explores and values ideas over aesthetics

Graffiti: Banksy and Jean-Michel Basquiat elevated graffiti from a form of vandalism to a form of art

Junk Art: popularized by Marcel Duchamp and Kurt Schwitters, junk art uses found objects and "junk" to make works of art

Feminist Art: highlights the social differences between women and men, associated especially with Judy Chicago and Nancy Spero

Land Art: popularized by Robert Smithson and Andy Goldsworthy, such art uses natural elements of the outdoors to create art works

Performance Art: associated with Marina Abramovich, such art combines visual art with performance, typically done by the artist

Installation Art: transforms a physical site and is sometimes ephemeral, disappearing before the next show

Digital Art: uses digital technology in the creation of works of art

I've probably missed many that flew under my art radar. Phew! You would think I would be delighted at this melange of creative options, but I am merely bewildered. Within my own lifetime, I have had to consider whether any of the above fit into my old-fashioned idea of art. Still, to help me move toward a definition of art, I jotted down some of the art works that I have seen or read about in the last few decades:

Marcel Duchamp hung a urinal on a gallery wall. It was entitled *Fountain*.

Jean Arp tore up bits of paper and fixed them where they fell.

Damien Hirst poured paint on a spinning machine and produced "spin paintings."

Jackson Pollock threw paint randomly on a canvas.

Shozo Shimamoto threw whole bottles of paint at canvases.

Andy Warhol stacked plywood Brillo boxes. He also urinated on canvases.

Piero Manzoni produced an edition of tin cans that each contained thirty grams of his own excrement (at least half of the purchased cans exploded).

Yves Klein once showed a completely empty gallery room as a work of art.

Tracey Emin showed an unmade bed as an art piece.

Marc Quinn made a head out of nine pints of his own frozen blood. It's rumored that an assistant at the Saatchi Gallery accidentally unplugged the bloody head and it started to melt!

Andy Galsworthy and **Robert Smithson** made ephemeral land art happenings from earth, trees, rocks, and leaves.

Walter De Maria planted four hundred stainless steel rods in a one mile by one kilometer field—that is how its dimensions are presented everywhere.

Jean-Michel Basquiat, Shepard Fairey, and **Banksy** painted graffiti on buildings.

Dennis Oppenheim patterned his body with sunburn.

Yoko Ono sat on a chair and invited the audience up to cut away bits of her clothing.

Damien Hirst made a diamond-encrusted skull, which bears the title given by his mother when she first saw it—*For the Love of God!* He also created a stuffed shark, *The Physical Impossibility of Death in the Mind of Someone Living*; it sold for twelve million dollars. His spot series are canvases covered in dots painted by his assistants.

Grayson Perry provocatively decorated urns and vases.

Yayoi Kusama is called the princess of polka dots because she decorated whole rooms with objects covered in polka dots.

I am a reasonable person and am willing to consider all

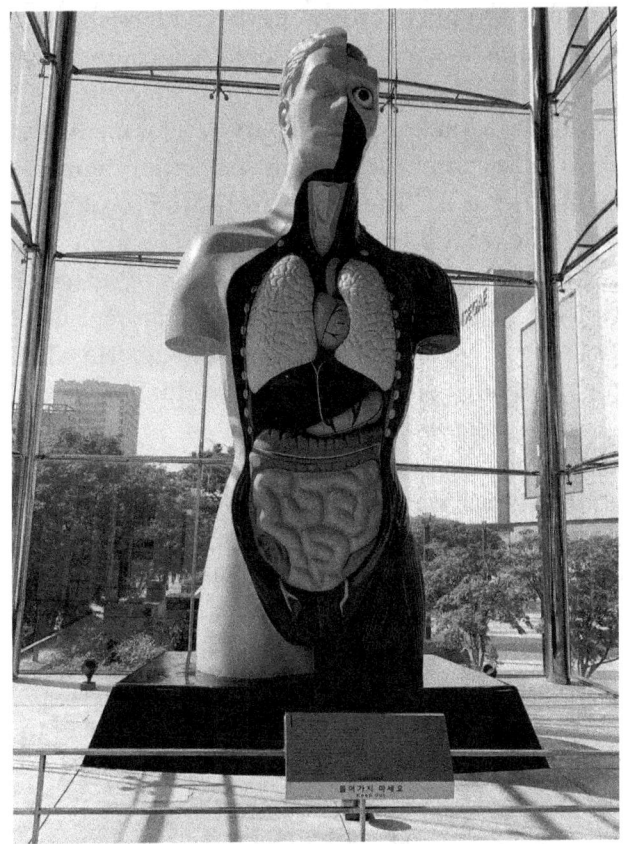

Hymn by Damien Hirst is often discussed as a key example of boundary-blurring between mundane reality and art.

the above under the heading "art." But how to link them all, give them a common banner they may all fly under? Perhaps a good first step toward some commonality would be to consider the function of art as well as its qualities.

Surely art is about beauty. It's an appreciation of balance, harmony, and rhythm. But beauty is such a relative word itself, depending as it does on familiarity.

Is art about truth? Philosopher Martin Heidegger said, "Art is the becoming and happening of truth." Truth is not necessarily beautiful, that's for sure. But maybe truth is a factor in the creation of a work of art. French sculptor Auguste Rodin also spoke about art needing to be truthful:

"There is nothing ugly in art except that which is without character, that is to say that which offers no outer or inner truth."

Art could be a kind of evolutionary development that helps us deal with the complexities of life. As author George Perec rather stiltedly put it, "The aim of art [is] to provoke in the beholder some reaction that reduced his alienation from the world, to build bridges between the self and the other." Alain de Botton also felt that art's mission is "the promotion of a sensory understanding of what matters in life." He felt art should change how we experience the world. Is art's role then to make some sense out of our world?

Art historian Ernst Gombrich suggested that "art is an institution to which we turn when we want to feel a shock of surprise. We feel this want because we sense that it is good for us once in a while to receive a healthy jolt. Otherwise we would so easily get stuck in a rut and could no longer respond to the new demands that life is apt to make on us. The biological function of art, in other words, is that of a rehearsal, a training in mental gymnastics which increases our tolerance of the unexpected." Jean Dubuffet accentuated the shock value when he said, "We expect art to uproot us, to unhinge doors." Well, yes, shocking does seem to be a function of art, at least recent art, where all our moral values, everything we have ever held sacred, seem up for assault. Our prejudices, our illusions, the supposed wisdom that our heritage has imparted to us . . . all shattered like sugar glass. Novelist Heather Jessup, in her Ph.D. dissertation, accentuated this assault when she listed the fundamental roles of art: "to fool viewers into insights, to trick patrons into mindful contemplation and to instill awareness into our habitualized assumptions or orientations." Is art's function then to break through our habitual reactions and make us more aware of our surroundings? Should art help us engage in a positive way with things unfamiliar to us?

Tolstoy opted for art being a sharing of emotions between creators and their audience. Denis Dutton supported this, having said, "Emotional pills will never replace art, because nothing can substitute for a sense of emotional expression derived from the experience of a complex aesthetic structure created by another human being." He felt art "springs from a desire for knowledge of another person."

Art does seem to be a language used by artists to connect their thoughts and emotions with their brushes and paints and chisels and computers in order to further this personal dialogue to embrace a wider audience, and they use their craft skills to do this. But even if works of art don't communicate with anyone, don't resonate with anyone, they could still resonate with the artists that produced them; the works could be a form of catharsis for them. Could art then be a type of therapy, playing a role in our emotional and psychological growth? Is art to compensate for our gaps? The clinical neuroscientist Raymond Tallis seemed to agree: "Art is expressing one's universal wound—the wound of living a finite life of incomplete meanings."

Denis Dutton summed up some qualities that he felt a work should have before it is called art. It should "give pleasure; exhibit skill and virtuosity; have a recognizable style (according to rules of composition and expression); display novelty (surprise) and creativity; represent different realities; have a focus that is unlike ordinary life; express individuality; express emotion; meet an intellectual challenge (with a complex answer); fit into art traditions and institutions; and most important, provide an imaginative experience for both artist and audience." These characteristics of art tie in nicely with those of Hans Prinzhorn, who collected art created by the institutionalized: art should be "expressive, decorative, playful, imitative, imposing order and giving the thing portrayed symbolic significance."

But am I any closer to a definition that suits me? These days, with the art market gone berserk as wealthy collectors drop millions for branded works, to arrive at a clear definition seems less and less likely. As they make markets for themselves, artists have to be entrepreneurs as well as innovators, for God forbid they do not produce something novel with each phase of their production—something novel that works as their brand. Branded artists need branded collectors, such as Charles Saatchi, David Geffin, Steve Cohen, or Adam Sender. Their works need to be seen in branded shows such as Art Cologne, The Volta Show, or Art Basle, and at branded galleries such as the Museum of Modern Art, the Guggenheim, or the Tate. Most of all, in order to have their brand fully recognized, artists need to have a piece sell for millions at a branded auction house such as Christie's or Sotheby's. Of auction houses, art sociologist Sarah Thornton said, "Even if the people here tonight were initially lured into the auction room by the love of art, they find themselves participating in a spectacle where the dollar value of the work has slaughtered other meanings."

Andy Warhol was perhaps the most blatant predecessor who linked art production with money-making; he even had a show of large canvases with only dollar signs painted on them. Warhol also launched "fame" as an art form. Does this make Paris Hilton and the Kardashians artists then, I wonder? Are today's artists more concerned with their own images than the images they are producing?

And then there is Artspeak, that peculiar language used by art writers. Japanese conceptual artist On Kawara did a series of paintings consisting solely of the date of the day the work was painted, done in white on a black background. Thornton noted that Christie's catalogue presented these paintings as "an existential statement, a proof of life." What can I say! Of an arrangement of 355 pounds of wrapped candies, curator Nancy Spector wrote, "The simple elegance of the work invites contemplation, even reverie." Artspeak is a whole other vocabulary—"cutting edge" (radical), "challenging" (impossible to explain), "museum-quality" (expensive). Of Yves Klein's solid blue canvases, Christie's catalogue said, "These works allow the viewer to bathe in the infinite, in the luminous spiritual world of the Blue . . . windows into the eternal and endless world of the spiritual realm." Well, I suppose that's possible. Curator Virginia Button, writing of Hirst's stuffed shark, stated, "Brutally honest and confrontational, he draws attention to the paranoiac denial of death that permeates our culture." An open coffin with the

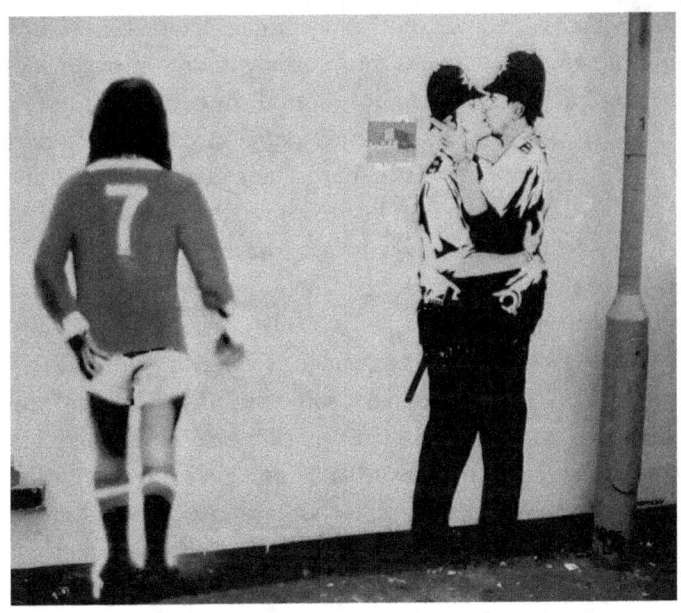

The Kissing Coppers is one of Banksy's best-known images.

corpse looking alive and well (thanks to cosmetics) might have been a more direct (and cheaper) artistic display for making this point, one would have thought. The seriousness given to conceptual art, happenings, and installations made critic John Carey declare of an exhibit at a Liverpool Biennial, "Another exhibit was a maze made out of cotton. It occupied a whole gallery, and was said to evoke 'the historical suffering of slavery.' In fact, reading even a short article on Liverpool and the slave trade would tell you more about the historical suffering of slavery than a cotton maze. But reading is comparatively arduous, whereas wandering around a cotton maze is just the kind of slipshod, superficial substitute for knowledge and understanding that conceptual art's advocates imagine themselves struggling against."

Art does seem to be more connected to the community these days, breaking out of those white cubes of galleries. Outdoor art has no entrance fee, no doors to go through, and it is often placed in marginalized places to reinvent them and to speak more readily to marginalized people. What has caused this? Maybe our increasing awareness of AIDS, homelessness, racism, classism, money inequalities, lack of freedom of expression, environmental concerns, and illiteracy make "pure" art seem like an indulgence and has caused art projects to move outside the mainstream art world, not just to give it wider viewership, but to allow it to become more involving, often asking the viewer to participate in the art process. Artworks are no longer just objects on display, and this frees them from the demands of the art market.

Until the seventeenth century, any acquired skill was considered an art. Britannica Online defines art as "the use of skill and imagination in the creation of aesthetic objects, environments, or experiences that can be shared with others." This definition originates from the Latin, where "ars" means "skill" or "craft." Andy Warhol caught the drift here when he defined an artist as "anyone who was good at what he did." That would cover almost everything produced imaginatively since man, or woman, scratched on cave walls.

Art, as most lay people would define it today, is art works created from the seventeenth to the early twentieth centuries, a time when the word "art" had limited application and usually referred to the fine arts of sculpture and painting, with the philosophy of aesthetics being attached. In the nineteenth century, everyone knew what a work of art was; when it wasn't showing the gods in their various forms, it was strictly showing reality as accurately as it could—until photography usurped that role. In a kind of defense against the threat of this new form, art withdrew, as it were, and moved to modernism, where it explored the nature of the medium itself, as if taking a closer look at its own very existence. Art was about art. Abstract expressionism was almost a mystic exploration of materials. But after Jackson Pollock's drippings, Andy Warhol's stacked plywood Brillo boxes and, more recently, Damien Hirst's stuffed shark, we've almost come full circle, as art has crashed through any remaining boundaries and broken all previous definitions of what it might be. As John Carey declared, "My answer to the question 'What is a work of art?' is 'A work of art is anything that anyone has ever considered a work of art, though it may be a work of art only for that one person.'" Some art can only be appreciated by its creator, some only by friends and family, some by a small coterie of people attached to a certain school of art, some by a much wider art audience, and some by the whole world. Supposing the metaphor the artist has used works for someone, surely that would be an inclusive way of considering a creation as a work of art.

I rather like my own most recent and moderately positive theory about what art might be. Certainly, it seems to me that the division between "high art" and "low art" is disappearing. Technology is enabling everyone to be a creator, and virtual and actual reality are becoming blended and confused, so almost every action can be defined somehow as art. It might well just be stated then that *art is the awareness of sensory action and reaction in the everyday*. In other words, *art is life lived awarely*.

Herbert Read is on my side here: "Every man is a special kind of artist and in his originating activity, his work or play, he is doing more than express himself: he is manifesting the form which our common life should take, in its unfolding." That is, art may be returning to its original meaning of a body of skills and information that effects change in matter.

The term "fine arts" is obsolete. If this is so, then "the arts" as we have known them in the past are in some way now denied a separate category from life in general. Art is asking that you become more aware in the everyday—aware of how you take out the garbage and how you wash the tines of a fork. Yes, as far as what art is, I do think I have something here, don't you?

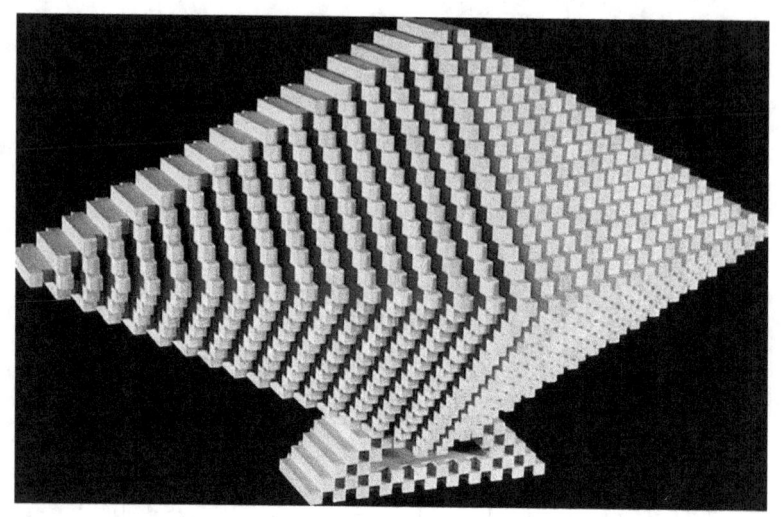

Elias Wakan, *Sliced Ice*

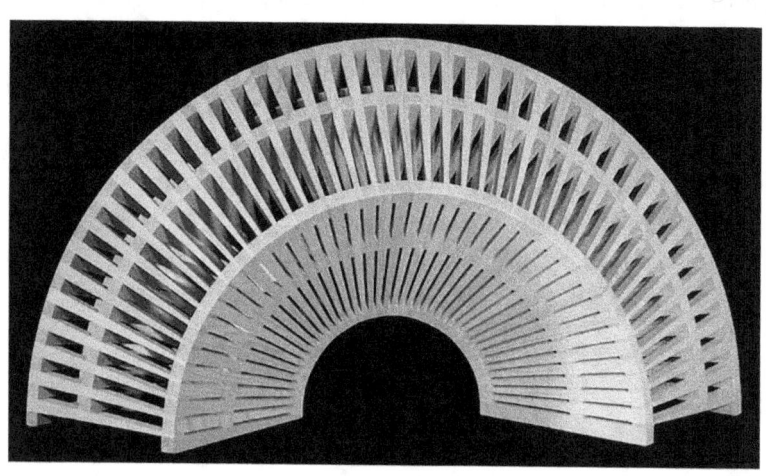

Elias Wakan, *Segue*

the creative process

If you want to increase your creativity, get out of your own way.
  —Robertson Davies

A creative life is itself a creation.
  —Elias Wakan

WELL, I CERTAINLY COVERED WIDE GROUND IN MY
search for a definition of art and the possibilities of what its
function might be. Perhaps now I can be a little more succinct
in searching for some boundaries to define the creative act
itself.

"My head is filling up with pictures just waiting to jump
onto the canvas." So said Georgia O'Keeffe, and anyone who
has created anything knows this feeling well. Sometimes the
creative idea jumps out fully formed, as Athena from Zeus's
forehead. More often it hangs around a while inside, as for
O'Keeffe.

I often wonder why artists procrastinate so when the
images are piling up inside their heads. It happens to
me, too, and I am very conscious of this. Are we holding
back, terrified that our next creation will not exceed in
excellence our last one? Or are we afraid we won't have the
energy to complete the creative impulse once it does start to
materialize?

Procrastination in the creative act is so strange. Sculptor
Stephen De Staebler commented, "Artists don't get down to

work until the pain of working is exceeded by the pain of not working." And yet for most of us, when we do relax—step aside as it were and let the creative energy flow—is there anything quite like it for pleasure? It's true we sometimes fear the creative urge will burst upon us and sweep us away, breaking us open with its tsunami-like strength. Science writer Jonah Lehrer described this urge as "the uncontrollable rush of creative insight, that flow of associations that can't be held back." It's as if we put our very life on the line every time we start a new work. But that's the way it is when your art and your life have become one.

It was hard enough exploring what art might be, but it seems almost impossible to define creativity. There are so many definitions that it's hard to choose which one might be correct; maybe they all contain elements of truth. Take poet Brewster Ghiselin's attempt: "The creative process is the process of change, of development, of evolution, in the organization of subjective life." This definition speaks not at all of the object resulting from the process but of the actual transformation of the artist and the environment around the artist. As Jung said, "It is not Goethe who created Faust, it is Faust that created Goethe." Jung felt that because the creative process comes from the unconscious, it might not be possible to explain it fully.

But then there's Bob Dylan's much simpler definition, "creativity is love and theft," which puts it all on a much more practical level. Dylan looked for a sound that "touches the bone," picked it up wherever he found it and ran with it. David Hume offered the following definition of creativity: "All this creative power of the mind amounts to no more than the faculty of compounding, transposing, augmenting, or diminishing the materials offered to us by the senses and experience." In other words, it's all there already; we just have to connect it up.

If we start by considering the very beginnings of the creative act, we find that the first strange and often confused feelings of excitement can build up to American scholar John Livingstone Lowes's "surging chaos of the unexpressed." Here we have the ill-defined yearnings, the vague idea, glimpses of an image. It can feel like boredom, but with a strange distant tug. It's as if a passing phrase we have read germinates inside us; the sound of distant bells stirs up an image; two colors oddly juxtaposed stay with us and dive underground to fertilize each other.

I remember clearly a moment in Myanmar when I chanced to see monks' robes of saffron and dark red thrown casually over a bright yellow wall. The impact was immediate, and yet I have still done nothing with it years later, just letting it ferment until it is ready. How will it manifest? I wonder. As a poem? An essay? A shifting of pillows on a couch?

There may be a problem to be solved running around in your head, and a vague feeling may be the germ of an answer. Even though it is only a hint, a slight feeling at this moment, it still must be noted if it is to manifest at all. There is a heightened awareness that something is happening. Yet it can't be grabbed or looked fully in the eye, for like a pixie, it will vanish immediately if you try to confront it. One has to stay in an almost trance-like state, an unfocused, eyes-half-closed state, giving the creative impulse time to pace itself. This incubation period may last minutes, days, or years. It demands patience on the part of the creator until things become clearer, for the conscious can handle the known, but not the unknown. It is almost as though the artist has to step aside and surrender to the process. Too much forcing or use of one's conscious will result in a sadly misshapen birthing.

I have just found a wonderful example of how the creative mind works while reading *Amsterdam*, by Ian McEwan. I came across a description of a composer in the process of composing: "forging it out of the call of a bird, taking advantage of the alert passivity of an engaged creative mind . . . It came as a gift; a large grey bird flew up with a loud alarm call as he approached. As it gained height and wheeled away over the valley it gave out a piping sound on three notes which he recognized as the inversion of a line he had already scored for a piccolo. How elegant, how simple. Turning the sequence round opened up the idea of a plain and beautiful song in common time which he could almost hear."

Creative urges demand expression though, for if not expressed, they will fester inside and do damage. However, as Jonah Lehrer commented, "The feeling of frustration—the act of being stumped—is an essential part of the creative process." Blocks are good. When one is blocked, the left hemisphere of the brain starts looking for answers. As Paul Valéry said, "A person is a poet if his imagination is stimulated by the difficulties inherent in his art and not if his imagination is dulled by them." Blocks are therefore necessary, but they should not be too impenetrable. When one is at an impasse, feeling frustrated, it is good to go into the garden and prepare a deeply dug asparagus bed. As Rollo May put it, "You go through a period of intense work, confront all the dilemmas, conflicts and blocks, then put it aside and let the unconscious do the work." Why not view the block as part of the incubation time necessary for the creative process? That is a much more positive view, and taking it may well stave off minor depression. (The final chapter of this book deals with the experience of being blocked.)

Encouraging creativity, then, seems to be a matter of balance. We need to stay in a dreamy, non-focused state, and yet, at the same time, we also need to be able to focus, for when we are focused, more information is sent to the prefrontal cortex for us to process. This is the area of our short-term memory where we can unconsciously sort out ideas to make connections. However, although this area will help with the processing and editing of our creative ideas, the epiphanies come from the right hemisphere. It's disillusioning, but as Jonah Lehrer said, "The imagination is transformed from something metaphysical—a property of the gods—into a particular twitch of the cortex." And yet, whatever this imagination is, somehow, as Anthony Julius so nicely stated, "Artists are imagination's representatives in that foreign country that is the external world."

To repeat, because it is important, our daydreaming must not be desultory; we must somehow be alert while we're daydreaming so we can catch an inventive idea when it appears. And when it does, Gabriel García Márquez expressed the next stage so well: "I don't see [inspiration] as a state of grace, nor as a breath from heaven, but as the moment when, by tenacity and control, you are at one with your theme. . . . You spur the theme on and the theme spurs you on too. All obstacles fade away, all conflict disappears, things you never dreamt of occur to you, and at that moment, there is absolutely nothing in the world better than writing."

To solve problems we need both divergent thinking—a flooding of spontaneous epiphanies—and convergent thinking—a selection of relevant input. However, though daydreaming may be the hook that encourages the creative image to appear, it is technique and discipline—the day-after-day futile brushstrokes on the canvas, the pounding out of words on the computer, the moving of one's hands over the keyboard—that eventually draws the creative impulse into full daylight. And when the image is clearer, it is then that the will comes into play to pin it down and revise and reorganize it. At that time, knowledge of your medium and skill in applying that knowledge helps the creative process along. We must have the skills, the techniques to change the insights into the creative object—music, painting, poetry, dance, etc.—before the creative act is brought to completion.

The creative object thus produced must have a viewer, that is, it must be recognized by others. John Carey stated, "A simplistic theory of the artistic process assumes that the artist feels an emotion, and then puts it into an artwork in such a way that the eventual viewer, or listener, or reader will take the same emotion out at the other end, rather like someone opening a parcel and feeling what the artist felt." Yes, that idea is a little too naive, for while it is true that this conscious molding of the creative impulse must be such that the viewer, the reader, the listener is able to recapture something of the first alertness, of the first emotions that the creator had at the start of the whole process, something of that first intense excitement that an undetermined, earth-shaking thing was about to take place, it doesn't always happen that way. Moreover, what we often feel is earth-shaking may, when it pops out, be of mouse-size significance. But you know, it doesn't matter whether it is like the world-shaking ideas of Einstein or merely small shifts in your own psyche; it is all creativity. What is earth-shaking about the creative act is that something new is appearing, some linking of ideas, concepts, images that has never happened before, at least not to you. The creative person is a revolutionary, an "edge" person, in that anything new threatens to overthrow old views. The creative person must step outside their own limits to allow in the fresh and the unexpected.

Yet it is not novelty alone that fully defines the creative act, but the gaining of fresh insight. The true manifestation shows in the turning around within the artists themselves, and if they are lucky, the turning around for the better in the environment around them.

By the way, the use of drugs and alcohol is not the way to encourage the creative impulse to emerge from the frustrated artist. Drugs may increase the dopamine in the brain, thus aiding connections, but the side effects aren't worth it. Drugs are a shortcut, but ideas that come by using them can so easily flood into a mess of useless junk. What among the junk is worth preserving? After a night overflowing with ideas, someone I know once said with a large sigh, "Stoned again!" Truman Capote commented on Kerouac's gigantic flood of drug-driven words in *On the Road*, "that isn't writing, it's typing."

Form, oddly enough, often stimulates creativity. Jonah Lehrer feels that familiarity with form is important in creativity, or at least in the creation of poetry, for "unless they [poets] are forced to look beyond the obvious associations, they'll never invent an original line. They'll be stuck with clichés and conventions, with predictable adjectives and boring verbs. When a poet needs to find a rhyming word with exactly three syllables, or an adjective that fits the iambic scheme, he ends up uncovering all sorts of unexpected connections: the difficulty of the task accelerates the insight process." And it is these "connections" that are the essence of creativity.

One needs persistence, however, in order to stay with the problem until insights connect. We can't just expect them to connect on their own; we have to work to link them. The muses may come, but they usually come when the welcome mat is made ready for them. As David Rakoff, that wonderfully critical commentator on mankind's woes, so pointedly said, "The only thing that makes one an artist is making art. And that requires the precise opposite of hanging out; it is the deep, lonely and unglamorous task of tolerating oneself long enough to push something out." And luckily, when it comes to connections, Lehrer noted, "At any given moment, the brain is automatically forming new associations, continually connecting an everyday x to an unexpected y." The ability needed, he felt, is "to be able to conceptually blend, i.e., to have separate ideas existing at the same time in the mind. The skill is to see the overlaps, how the two ideas can combine."

As they arrive, new connections demand disciplined channeling, not a running wild in hallucinatory fashion. After the first burst, an intense concentration, skilled technique, and a few rules are what is needed for a successful conclusion to the act. The danger is that the revision, the reordering of the creative material may blot out the first spontaneous strokes on the canvas, the first joyous phrase on the page, first theme jotted down on the staff. There is the danger of over-writing, over-painting that first glorious creative moment.

And when the canvas is complete, the music written, the story down, is the creative idea still there? Does the finished piece fully express what the creator wanted to say, or has he or she lost the thread? They say that the moment you open your mouth, you lie; and that may be true of writing, painting, and composing too. Is the gap between that original impulse and what is completed too great? Do they ever completely match? As poet Stanley Kunitz stated, "The poem in the head is always perfect." Somehow, it is as if the creative tide of inspiration, having swept the beach, recedes and takes something of itself back with it. The moment the word hits the page or the brush the canvas, there is a certain wobble off-course.

Still, the editing process is just as important to the creative act as the inspirational moment. Milton Glasser, the inventor of "I ♥ NY," said, "I think people need to be reminded that creativity is a verb, a very time-consuming verb. It's about taking an idea in your head, and transforming that idea into something real. And that's always going to be a long and difficult process. If you're doing it right, it's going to feel like work." David Rakoff was rather more positive and lyrical about this moment. He said, "Fraught and messy though an artistic life may be, is there a drug that can induce the euphoria as energizing as that intensely fragile moment when the muse passes through one, and the artist becomes the simultaneously perfect and flawed instrument of expression?"

People seem to have a variety of optimum times for receiving creative ideas. For me it is in the afternoon when I lie reading material in a desultory sort of way (cartoonist David Langdon called it "controlled mind-wandering") and the ideas just flow out and I jot them down. The best time for me to edit and restructure notes is in the early morning when my brain is alert. However, sometimes waking from a dream, the poem or essay comes up almost fully formed. Awareness is essential for me when waking in the morning, for that's also the time creative ideas often slip out. Whatever the optimum time for you, however, a period of quiet time is necessary (keeping busy kills creativity), and what is also necessary is a quiet space. You need to make an oasis for yourself, however small it may be. A room of one's own.

And where do these inspirational ideas, images, and sounds come from? As Leonard Cohen so nicely said, "If I knew where the good songs come from, I'd go there more often." The argument as to whether the creative act is truly a creating or just a reproducing of something from the great storehouse in the sky has been going on since ancient times. I feel, but do not know for sure, that healthy beings are continually self-organizing. Out of that continual process come moments that demand a manifestation in the external world for completion—an action, a decision, an invention, a poem, a painting, a piece of music—something to anchor the process in reality, something to signal that a healthy shift has happened.

A creative person—is there such a type? A solemn, self-important person who feels they are irreplaceable is rarely the creative type. Oddly enough, ignorance and innocence seem to allow for a facility of fresh expression where more knowledgeable creators hesitate, aware of the hazards ahead. When it comes to naiveté, Steve Martin described it so well, "Despite a lack of natural ability, I did have the one element necessary to all early creativity—naiveté, that fabulous quality that keeps you from knowing just how unsuited you are for what you are about to do." Along with naiveté often goes a sense of wonderment at our complex universe.

John Cleese said, "Creativity is not a talent, it is a way of operating. In open mode, everything is a clue." Creativity has little to do with intelligence. It is a facility for getting into a mood, often a playful one. Yes, the ability to play is a key, yet it must somehow be *directed* play. As John Cage noted, "Art consists of purposeless play, charged with the imperative of waking us up to the very life we're living."

A creative person tends to be a person full of curiosity for its own sake, not single-mindedly goal-directed. A creative person is able to allow fresh ways of viewing the world, for if one is too rigid in outlook, nothing will appear. A creative person often has an inability to focus totally in one subject area. This is actually an advantage, for it means that they are then able to let more of the world in. A relaxed mind will also encourage an increase in alpha waves, which apparently indicate inspiration is happening. The neural parallel of insight is a load of activity in the anterior superior temporal gyrus—in the right hemisphere just above the ear. The steady signal of alpha waves from the right hemisphere is what promises insight. This process is what has been tested in labs, but it still hasn't solved the mystery of how inspiration really happens. A creative person, for various reasons, does seem to have easier access to the brain's unconscious processes.

A creative being has to have some kind of self-confidence that they can pull off the creative act, even though doubt appears each time. One has to be willing to take risks, willing to fail time and time again, yet somehow have faith that failing will eventually produce a success. Sometimes you have to trust your intuition when it tells you that your insight is workable. If you're worried about mistakes, you'll never produce anything. As cartoonist Scott Adams said, "Creativity is allowing yourself to make mistakes. Art is knowing which to keep." And American artist John Baldessari reminded us, "Art comes out of failure." When those creative ideas are flowing, none of them are wrong, perhaps just wrong for that particular project.

Some people say one needs to be buoyant and happy in order to create, while others note their best successes are in times of dire distress when all that can be offered is a surrendering to the situation or a stark crying out in despair. A happy mood may encourage inspiration, but a little sadness can sharpen our awareness and help the editing phase. I am told that writers are four times as likely as the general public to be manic-depressive. As Nancy Andreasen, one of the world's leading authorities on creativity, put it so succinctly, "If you're at the cutting edge, you're going to bleed." However, your load of ideas that arrive during the mania of your epiphanies can be sorted out in the relative calmness of your depression, so maybe being slightly (not clinically) manic-depressive is the perfect formula for a creative person. The manic mode allows for inspiration and the closed mode for reviewing, decision-making, and editing.

Certainly, a change in mood offers a momentary gap for the idea or the image to slip through. At times of transition we tend to be more vulnerable, less rigid, and thus more open to novel ways of looking at things. And being an outsider or working at the edge of your qualified field seems to be an advantage when it comes to creativity, for interesting things happen at boundaries. This may necessitate putting yourself in the position of being a foreigner, but an outsider's advantage is usually a state of mind rather than dwelling in the extremes of being a refugee or a stranger in a strange land.

Paradoxically, while it may be best to stand alone on the fringe for creativity to strike, working with others is also stimulating. However, the others you choose to involve must never be inhibiting with negativity but must be able to explore and further your insights positively.

What is so desirable about being a creative person? Doesn't it go against the idea of community responsibility that we concentrate on our own advantageous ends, our own expression of what we claim are our own ideas and images, our unique way of looking at the world? May not these acts of creation actually be counter to community interests?

Questions and yet more questions. Still the afternoon sun is sinking, and I am in a lethargic mood, and a most beautiful little poem idea has just popped into my head. I don't much care whether it is for my own good, the community's good, or the planet's good. I don't much care if it is my sole invention or has been plucked from the universal unconscious. I just love the feeling of the words rippling out in the right order . . . no need to justify, question, explain . . . just a full birth. Can one ask for more?

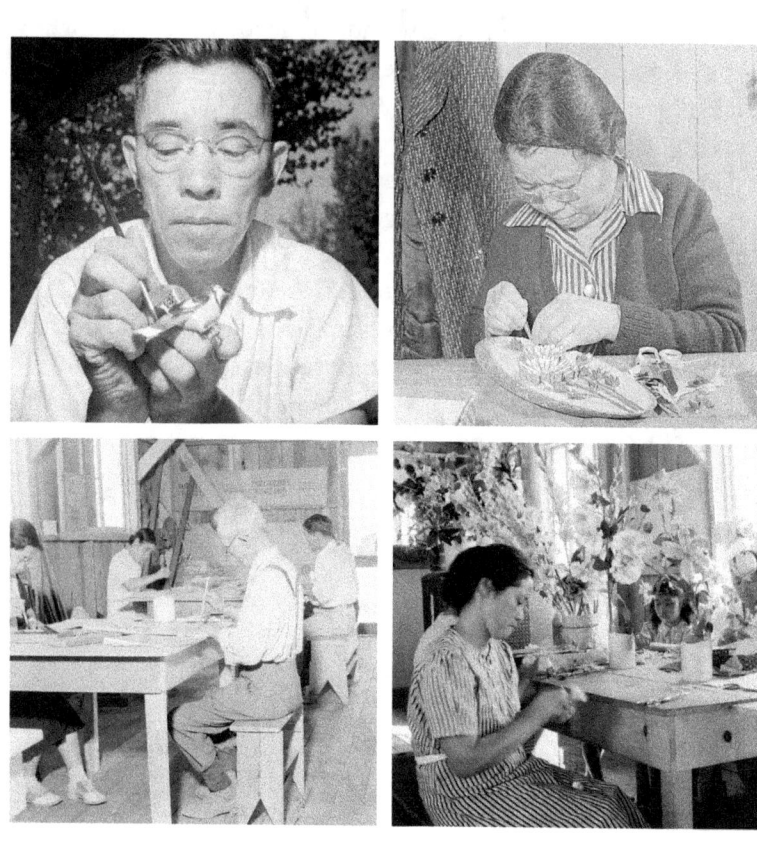

Evacuees of Japanese ancestry at work on art projects
at relocation centers during World War II

the art of
confinement

I LIVE ON A SMALL ISLAND. THE LIBRARY, POST OFFICE, and bank are at the opposite end from where I live, and I only venture there once a week. I can go a whole seven days without leaving our half-acre property, perfectly happy so long as my pen is flowing on paper or my fingers clicking on the keyboard. Taking the ferry to Vancouver Island, twenty minutes away, happened once every couple of months until I became Poet Laureate of Nanaimo when I had to go more frequently to read at civic events. Taking the two ferries necessary to get to Vancouver, on the mainland, is a very reluctant undertaking. My life, you might say, is one of voluntary confinement, though not totally that of a recluse.

J. D. Salinger, Thomas Pynchon, and Greta Garbo all wanted to be alone, and in the case of the first two, to be alone to create as a recluse. Emily Dickinson similarly chose voluntary confinement for her astonishingly productive poetic life and even stated, "To live is so startling it leaves little time for anything else." Many other creative people have set physical limits on their lives, such as Alan Moore, who described his condition this way: "I don't have any designs on being a screenwriter. For one thing, that would mean moving out of Northampton, and I already can't imagine that. I very seldom even leave this end of the living room. The other end of the living room is a foreign place where they do things differently, and where I feel a bit nervous." Boundaries are not necessarily destructive of the creative impulse and sometimes are even preferred in order to prevent distraction. Can we even live in this world without a few boundaries? I wonder.

But then there is creativity under inflicted confinement—as in the case of the forced confinement of Colette by her husband, Willy (Henry Gauthier-Villars), who kept her under lock and key for his own financial gain until she produced the four *Claudine* novels that he published under his own name.

Prison art is also produced under inflicted confinement, though here the artist has been declared guilty of some crime and so supposedly has caused his/her own restricted condition. Within confines, the ability to express oneself is limited by access to tools and materials. Still, a way must be found to validate oneself when one has been invalidated, even though it may have been self-inflicted. As Henry Ray Clark, a long-term prisoner, expressed it, "As long as my mind can create something beautiful to look at, I am a free man." As to limited materials, prisoner Raymond Materson swapped cigarettes for an old pair of socks. He unraveled them and started making the most detailed miniature tapestries.

Matchsticks, cardboard, magazines . . . whatever can be found in jails has been used for creative expression by someone. I have seen a photograph of dice made from toilet paper, water, and glue—not exactly fine art, but focused and inventive, nevertheless.

After the attack on Pearl Harbor, in a U.S. government panic, two-thirds of the existing 120,000 Japanese-Americans, all of whom were law-abiding American citizens, were evacuated to internment camps for fear they be saboteurs. The remaining third were Japanese nationals; they too were evacuated—though some returned to Japan—and were law-abiding as far as we know. A similar forced evacuation happened in Canada. The U.S. War Relocation Office saw the need for schools, churches, and libraries in these camps to prevent unrest among such large gatherings of people. The inmates contributed to the war effort by fulfilling government contracts. They were not threatened with death, though there

Gaman

And in the tar-paper shacks
with no tools at hand,
they forged chisels from bedsprings,
knives from abandoned animal traps,
and made string from old onion sacks.
And with these they shaped the impossible—
teapots from hard rock,
baskets from scrap papers.
They even made paintings on
the back of their own evacuation notices.
They taught their children to write
using chimney soot for ink,
and to type using letters cut circular
from old Sear's catalogues.
Their bitterness melted down
to make community,
their resignation sparked
into creativity—an insult
transmuted into art.
When humanity goes crazy
and fear overtakes reason,
it's folks with gaman
who laugh with lizards
and walk straight-backed
into the mists.

was barbed wire on the perimeter and soldiers stationed in watchtowers.

The history of those forced into internment camps in North America during World War II has been recorded in Delphine Hirasuna's well-illustrated book, *The Art of Gaman*. "Gaman" means self-denial as a supreme mark of valor. In the case of the internment camps, gaman meant staying silent, not speaking of losses, retaining dignity in the face of undeserved punishment.

Gaman is what kept this confined community solid. Yet in all the camps, it was the humiliation that required gaman and steered creativity as an outlet. Artists were provided with materials, although in some camps the very restrictive supply forced inventiveness. They scavenged items such as nails, used cigarette paper wrappings, packing crates, onion and gunny sacks, even plastic toothbrush handles. Since interns had not been allowed to bring scissors, hammers, or knives into the camps, they forged these from car springs, animal traps, and just about any discarded metal they could find. Wherever the camp was situated, local material found its way into their art—shells from a dry lake bed, ironwood, cactus, stones, slate, cypress root, tule reeds. For painters, recording the actual structures of the camp was a prevalent theme, although the buildings had to be shown in a positive light lest the camp officials think the works of art were negative propaganda.

But how about the artist's life under extreme confinement, with death ever present on the horizon? What happened to the Jews in German concentration camps before and during World War II was not just confinement, but a situation where the detainees were treated as vermin to be exterminated. As Peter Hayes wrote, "Auschwitz was, of course, the epitome of the Nazi industrialization of death, the place where the Third Reich established probably the largest human disassembly line that the world has ever known."

Granof, Mickenberg, and Hayes, in their large, copiously illustrated and heart-breaking book, *The Last Expression: Art and Auschwitz*, declared, "In many cases it is remarkable that the art . . . even survived, having been stored underneath floorboards, behind walls, tightly folded for hiding in clothes, or smuggled out of the camps. Made with unstable media, much of the art was neither well-preserved nor documented." Elsewhere, the authors stated, "Here art is used in the service of witnessing and to provide an outlet or cathartic avenue." But the art produced in the camps was not just cathartic or acting as a witness to the atrocities, for often survival depended on it. Art was a commodity that could be traded for food or for less harsh treatment by the guards.

In Auschwitz, as Alfred Cantor said, "Sketching took on a new urgency. . . . Even though I knew there was no chance to take these sketches out of Auschwitz, I drew whenever possible. . . . My commitment to drawing came out of a deep instinct for self-preservation and undoubtedly helped me to deny the unimaginable horrors of life at that time. By taking the role of observer, I could at least for a few moments detach myself from what was going on in Auschwitz and was therefore better able to hold together the threads of sanity."

Sybil Milton's remarks also appeared in *The Last Expression: Art and Auschwitz:* "In Auschwitz, canvas and paint were secreted from labor assignments in SS offices, kitchens, or on the black market that existed in every camp and ghetto. Drawings were made on the backs of SS circulars, reports, and medical forms, on wrapping paper, tissue paper, and even on reused paper pockmarked with bullet holes from SS target practice. Charcoal, rust, watered ink, food, and vegetable dyes often provided the raw materials for color, line, and texture. High-quality normal canvas and oils were available on occasion, particularly when an artist received a labor assignment in an art or technical barracks, or in an art forgery workshop." In the concentration camps, artistic outlets allowed the artists to express their individuality even when they had been denied their humanity. Portraits seemed to have been a common genre, perhaps giving a sense of permanence when the situation was so fragile.

Some artists may find their work limited by income or space, but still they remain human beings; they retain their menschness. Creating under extreme constraints inflicted by outside conditions, such as those in concentration camps, can hardly be imagined. A certain degree of gratitude should be expressed, perhaps daily, for the freedom to create. It is a priceless gift.

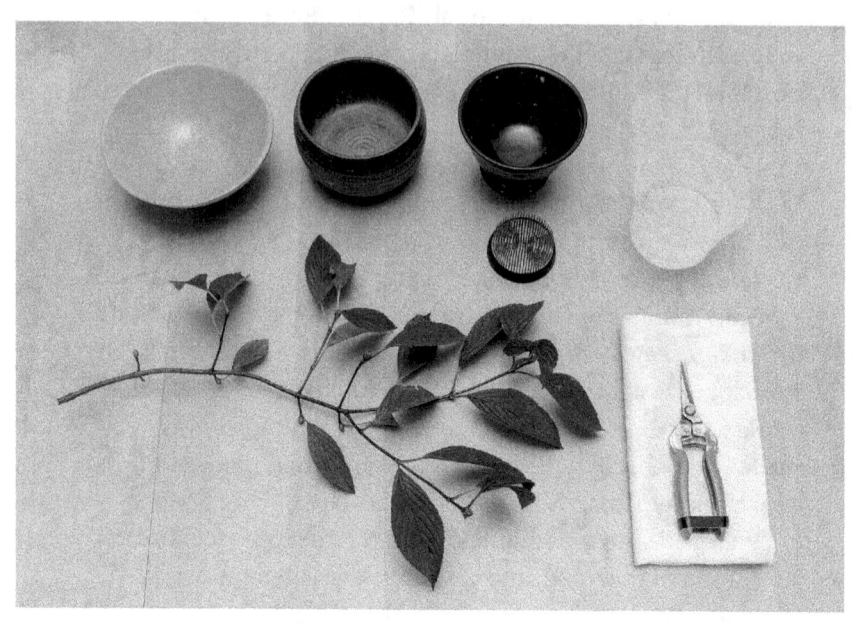

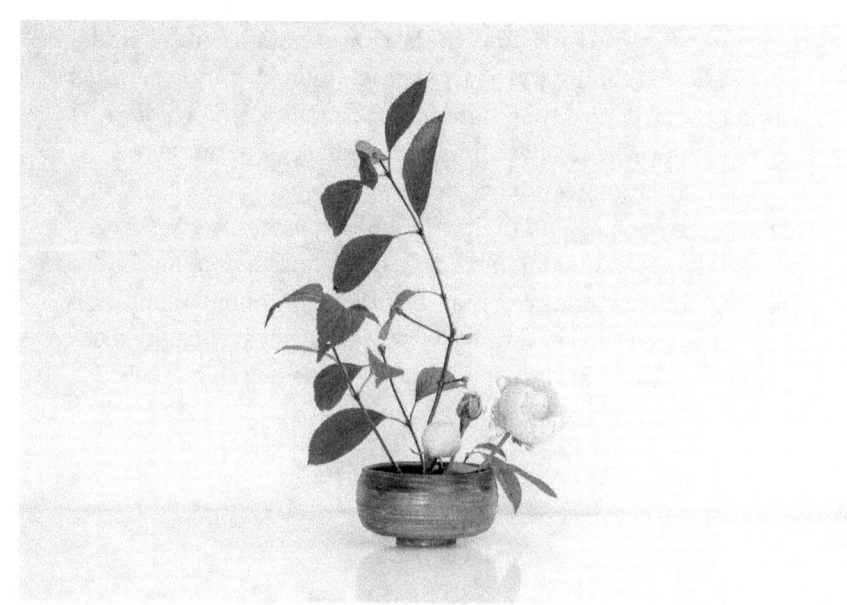

Ikebana by Henry Kellner

the art of
ikebana

I NEVER SAW MY FATHER AND MOTHER KISS OR embrace. My mother was sentimental, but lacked the ability to express real feelings; my father was remote. Yet when my father culled huge bouquets of flowers from his sensational herbaceous border and gave them into my mother's willing hands, it was enough for me to know there was a bond between them.

Oddly enough, I can't remember any of my mother's flower arrangements. What I do remember, however, is that after a storm, she would gently place dismembered flower-heads in a shallow bowl, a thing I continue to do to this day. I also remember her dealing with seed pods. The large seed pods of the poppy she would paint silver or gold and have them as winter decoration in the drawing room—a room seldom used because it was "for best." The other seed pod she handled was that of the honesty (known as silver dollar). The annual removal of the skins on either side of the central panel released the seeds and left the translucent center as a very decorative element in dried flower arrangements.

I may have inherited some elements of my mother's erratic cooking and housecleaning ways, but I definitely took on the mantel of her love of flowers. During my Japanese phase, I studied *ikebana*.

Kadō is a more formal word for "flower arrangement." Literally, it is "The Way of Flowers," "way (*dō*)" being the word used in the name of many traditional Japanese disciplined pursuits that are intended to result in personal inner development. Japanese schools for studying these pursuits often finish with the word "dō," for studying with a teacher is a "way" to develop yourself as a human being—a built-in benefit as you become trained in a discipline such as *aikidō* or *kendō* (both forms of martial arts), *shodō* (calligraphy), *kōdō* (incense appreciation) and, the subject of this essay, *kadō*.

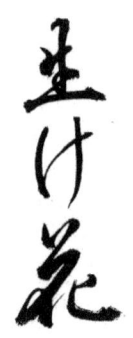

by Sonja Arntzen

Although I have had a few lessons and am not totally ignorant of the art of *ikebana*, I do find it hard to be really serious about anything involving a power structure, and there is certainly a power structure in the way *ikebana*—and many other arts—is taught in Japan. The structure is headed by an iemoto; students of an iemoto are much like disciples of a guru. The iemoto, it is believed, holds the secrets—the "known unknown"—of the respective art, and they are strict authoritarians. The iemoto system sounds ominous, but actually it's much like the multi-level system of companies like Avon. Excellent students become sub-teachers and enroll their own students. Sub-teachers give a portion of their income to their superior teachers, and so it goes until the iemoto gets the final cut. Each sub-teacher is certified, as is each student when they reach different stages of proficiency. They have to pay for this certification, which at the higher levels runs into millions of yen! This system is open to fierce rivalries between the schools, and nepotism, if not corruption, is not at all uncommon.

If my description of the iemoto system sounds negative, it is because I feel a topic should be presented in its entirety—warts and all. In the case of *ikebana*, it is best to get the negatives over with first. I speak of this rigid system not just as a warning, but also as an encouragement, for I want to assure you that you do not have to become an indentured student who has to study with a teacher for the rest of your life at great expense in order to understand the essentials of *ikebana*, which is, after all, the practice of studying flower arrangement as a way to enrich one's life. Once you grasp the basic principles, you can be off and away on your own. The necessary requisites are not teachers but rather practice and an opening of one's being to the life of flowers. I hope my introductory note will not discourage anyone from pursuing this wonderful "way."

Ikebana involves paradoxes, the most obvious one being that by cutting "live flowers"—the literal translation of *ikebana*—in order to recreate, in a vase, the setting from which one has cut them, one is actually hastening their death. Another paradox is that, although the Japanese love perfection, they also love a touch of imperfection—a crack in a vase, a well-worn gate, an irregularly thrown pot. Even in the most perfect arrangement, balance depends on three main elements, rather than the four one might assume when balance is under consideration. In traditional *ikebana*, an even number of branches is rarely used because, while balance is valued, a certain asymmetry is also appreciated. That is, one has to achieve balance and asymmetry at the same time. When it comes to balancing branches, four is considered an unlucky number in Japan, since "shi," the pronunciation of the word for "four," is the same as the word for "death."

Yet another paradox is that although the finished *ikebana* reflects the state of the practitioner—every time you place a branch, it is like a mirror showing you who you are—often the material available demands, by its shape, that it be used in a certain way; students have to subdue their own desires for the arrangement's desires and let it have its own way. So *ikebana* is not just about bringing nature into the home, but also about creating a link between human beings and nature, a balance between desires and reality.

Doing *ikebana* is somewhat like construction sculpture in that elements—plant material rather than metal, wood, or stone—are assembled and then set in the desired relationships to one another. Once constructed, the inessentials of the *ikebana* are clipped away, just as carving sculptors chip away at their stone or wood to reveal an essential shape that they have seen within. Just like sculpture, *ikebana* is concerned with size, shape, line, texture, volume, and, perhaps most importantly, negative space. The arrangement, as in the best sculpture, goes beyond mere attractiveness, for it is concerned with the emotion that has given rise to the piece. Again, just like sculpture needs its plinth to set it off, in *ikebana* the vase and even the base for the vase to stand on are integral parts of the whole design. Avant-garde *ikebana* is actually almost indistinguishable from sculpture, since plant material is often all but eliminated in its arrangements.

Each of the many schools of *ikebana* has its set rules, and here is another paradox: in some strange way, the rules allow students greater freedom to be able to offer a fresh way of viewing the material and, by extension, a fresh way of viewing life. (As suggested in the chapter on creativity, perhaps rules force the brain to make more unusual connections.) *Ikebana* is concerned with our relationship with nature (plant material), and through that exploration we can examine our relationship with all things.

Any material is open for use in *ikebana* practice, so paradoxically, one has to learn to discriminate among the many elements available and yet be non-discriminating, in that dead or wilted plant material may be just as suitable as the freshest.

Perhaps one of the biggest paradoxes in the history of *ikebana* was that in the seventeenth century—the golden age of the grand style of *ikebana*, called *rikka*—courtiers and influential samurai showed off their wealth by the immense size of their floral arrangements at the same time that they used simple tea rooms and the *nageire* style of *ikebana*, which supported spiritual solace.

When the tea ceremony developed fully in the sixteenth century, the flower arrangements for the tea room were much simpler than the *rikka* ones. Often only one flower was used. These simple *ikebana* were known as *chabana* (tea room flowers) or *nageire* (thrown in a pot) because they were much

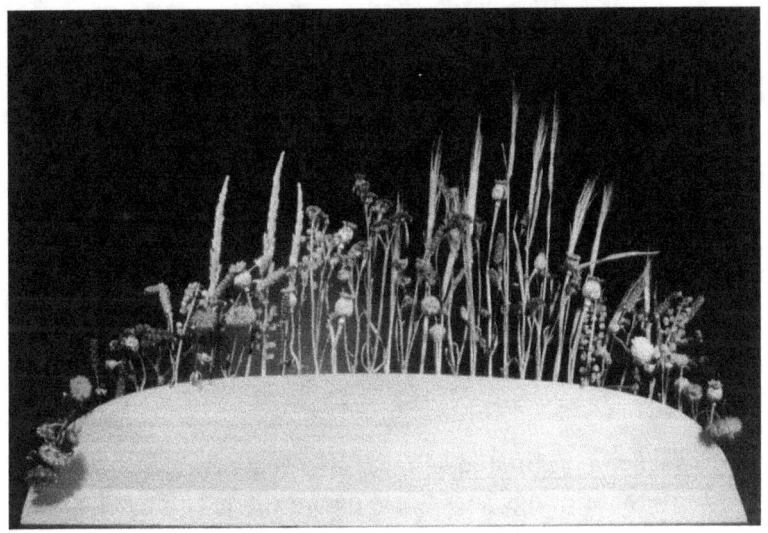

Elias Wakan, *Field of Dreams*

more relaxed when it came to rules of design and didn't need artificial supports, as did the large branches of the *rikka* arrangements. The vases for *chabana*, therefore, had narrow mouths to keep the material upright. Still, while simple, much care had to be given to *chabana*, as to the choosing of just the right container for the right flower, which should be set to be viewed at just the right angle.

The Japanese culture does seem to be riddled with paradoxes. Perhaps paradox is the essence of Zen—the ability to hold and blend two opposite ideas in one's mind at the same time.

Although the rules are complex, the actual tools needed for *ikebana* are of the simplest: a vase, a *kenzan* (pin holders, essential in low-dish-style *ikebana*), shears, wire cutters, and a syringe. Even for large outdoor *ikebana* when a chain-saw might sometimes be used, often a pair of Japanese scissors is sufficient. Any good book on *ikebana* will indicate how and when the flowers should be picked and prepared before the arrangement is started, such as cutting them in the early morning or early evening when the stems are full of sap. Books will also discuss the kinds of vases for each type of arrangement and the variety of bases that can be used in order to complete the display.

Although I started off rather negatively, decrying the indentured-student way that *ikebana* is taught in Japan, I am sensible enough to know that anything pursued with intensity can break one open. So, to end this chapter, please allow me to consider seriously the benefits of *ikebana* for its practitioner.

- The art of *ikebana* is an artistic exploration of space, proportion, line, color, and the balance of these factors.

- *Ikebana* originated as a way to placate the gods with floral offerings, and it has become a discipline to calm the destructive forces inside us. *Ikebana*, which is practiced in absolute silence, has a calming effect on the psyche. Worries have to be put aside as the arranging demands that the whole of one's being be focused during the process. The practice of art forms in Japan is often also a form of meditation, a way of stilling the ever-chattering mind. The state of mind achieved while practicing is as important as the art form.

- *Ikebana* is a way of communicating without words. One's emotions and ideas can all be conveyed by the way one chooses to do the *ikebana*.

- All Japanese arts are a way to give form to the formless, and *ikebana* certainly takes one beyond surface expression to a deeper kind of reality.

- *Ikebana* teaches the ephemeralness of all things, for the moment the stem is cut, the flower starts to fade.

- Working with the scents of the plant materials is a healing practice.

- Matching the arrangement to the season, one gets into the rhythm of life's cycles . . . the coming into being and the passing away. It helps one live in harmony with nature rather than at odds with it.

- As one learns the characteristics of each flower used, one develops an interest in the wonder of plant life.

I suppose enlightenment may be the aim of some *ikebana* masters. Stella Coe, a pioneer of the Sogetsu school in the West, described enlightenment in this way: "It is thinking about who you are that prevents you from seeing inwardly that you are. When you see with your inward eye that you are and that the world is beginning again and again, you are enlightened."

If you can sort that quote out, you will have dug to the essence of *ikebana* and, indeed, to the essence of all Japanese cultural disciplines.

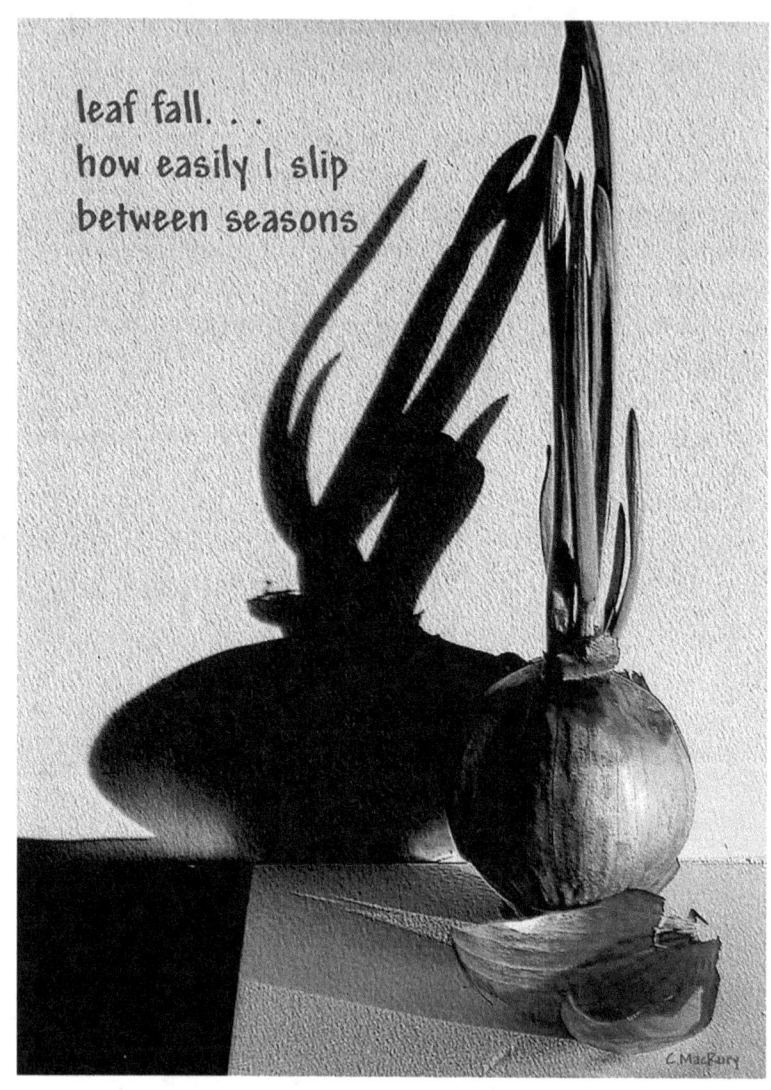

leaf fall. . .
how easily I slip
between seasons

Haiga by Carole MacRury

the art of
haiga

"BABBLE AND DOODLE ARE TWO OF THE MOST PRIMITIVE and universal human activities." So said Professor Leon Zolbrod. He was speaking specifically of the words of haiku and the strokes of haiga (the paintings that sometimes accompany haiku). Since the words and the strokes came from the same brush, so to speak, they naturally developed together.

Traditional haiga (predominately from the seventeenth through the nineteenth centuries in Japan) is a composite form of art, consisting of haiku, calligraphy, and brush painting. These are all paradoxical activities in that the poet's and painter's activities must be completely infused with concentration and vitality, yet somehow because of this intensity, the poet and painter disappear, and one is left with only a few words and a faint picture; no creator is present. It's as if in the concentrated moment, the words wrote themselves and the painting emerged subtly from the void.

The essence of the haiku and the haiga is, of course, spontaneity, immediacy. Not the immediacy of recording an emotion or an idea as it occurs but the images that have triggered them. Haiku and haiga are merely the recording of the senses. One brushes past a bush of lavender and releases its scent; one tastes the first plum of the year; one strokes a new baby's skin; one hears a temple bell in the distance; one glimpses a traveler far off on the road winding into the hills. Only sense impressions are called for.

In haiku, words are in the present tense because the here and now is being recorded. As Bashō, the great haiku poet, said, "as fast as an ax fells a tree, or a sword is drawn." The haiga, too, merely records the scene.

Such speed does not come without practice, although anyone can produce a haiku or a haiga if skillfully guided. To continually produce successful words and accompanying pictures takes years of trying and failing. The technique must be so embedded that it doesn't show. But besides technique, something else is required for a successful haiku, or haiga, and that is a state of innocence and clear seeing. Clear seeing—no separation between the writer and artist and their work, no separation giving time to put in details, to say how this is like that. There is only time to show how this is like this. There is no room for didactic statements, moral judgments, social comment. There is just a recording of a sensing moment.

Haiku and haiga exemplify the quality of wabi-sabi—sparseness, roughness, loneliness, brevity, simplicity. There is no overflowing of words or brushstrokes, merely a hint, and yet that hint needs nothing added or taken away for the reader or viewer to be able to catch the original emotion that triggered the work. The reader and viewer are also part of the creative act, remaining attentive to the overtones of the words and painting that ring out to the ends of the universe.

The open-endedness of the poem and picture is paradoxically what helps capture the moment. The past is implied and the next action hinted at, yet the words and painting only tell of the present. No wonder Zen monks were practitioners of these arts. The many mysteries of the universe are hinted at when a petal falling from a magnolia blossom is fully spoken of and illustrated.

Haiga and haiku are not neat things, not clever, polished, or sophisticated. The image is roughly captured, whether by words or paint. An eye is a slit, a nose a small curve, a mouth goes up or down to vaguely suggest joy, or sadness—and all this without effort. You can't try to paint a haiga using your intellect or when you are overwhelmed by emotions. In fact you can't "try" at all. Either the intensity that drives the brush is there, or it is not.

Traditional Japanese haiga were brushed beside the haiku, which often was written in one downward line. Today, outside Japan, many haiga are done with digital photographs. A far cry, you might say, from spontaneity as the photographer manipulates the image this way or that. And yet the best photo-haiga are equal in power

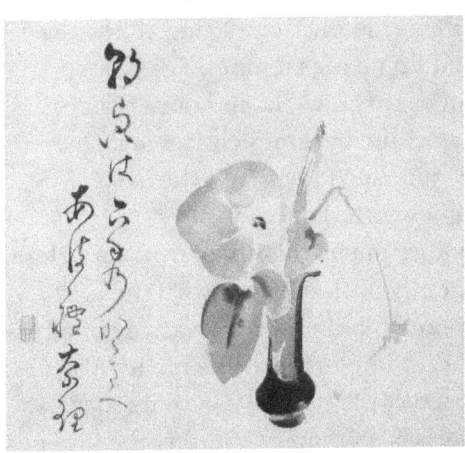

Haiga by Bashō, seventeenth century

to anything Buson might have painted. Here is a photo-manipulated haiga by the brilliant haiku and tanka writer Carole MacRury:

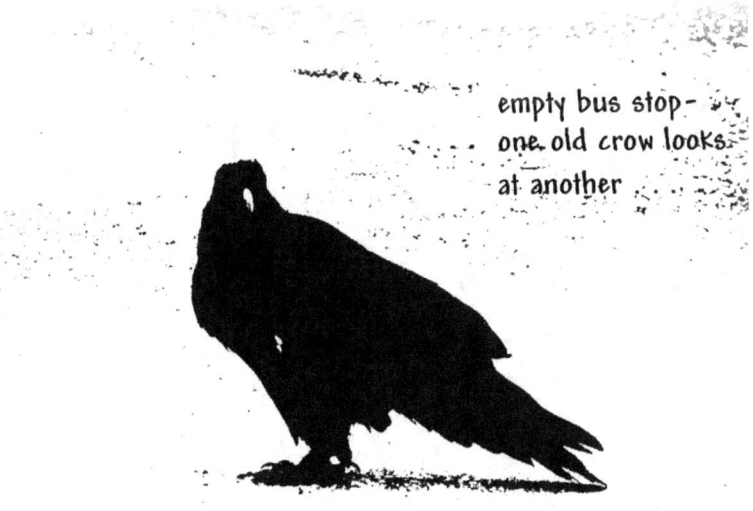

empty bus stop—
one old crow looks
at another

c.macrury

The two small glimpses of white within the feathers somehow make the black that much darker. No image of the other crow or the bus stop, yet somehow the simple image includes them both. And it also gives rise in the viewer to the idea that our journey in life is merely the waiting at a series of bus stops, that our fixed home is as temporary as a stop at a caravanserai, and that as we grow old and our feathers droop, this ephemeralness of life becomes clearer and clearer to us. Good haiga can produce such ideas and the usual accompanying sigh that goes with them.

Another haiga by MacRury opens this chapter (p. 52). Here the illustration has apparently nothing to do with the haiku, and yet the fallen skin of the onion marks the passing of all things, and the sharp shadow implies that this reality may not be all it seems to be. The idea of Plato's cave with its shadows merely reflecting reality arises, perhaps. Certainly the idea of multi-universes we might be able to "slip between" gives rise to endless questions.

Below is a haiga by Jim Swift who has developed photo-haiga to a fine art. This is an example of an abstract haiga that resonates so well with the accompanying haiku. There is a

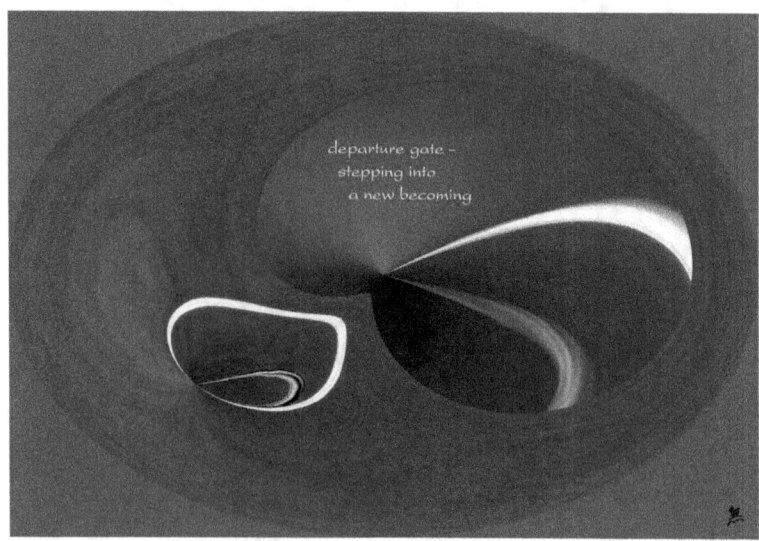

departure gate—/ stepping into / a new beginning

feeling of the coming and going at the airport, the excitement of new adventures. And yet here too is a feeling of cycles, of the possibility that our lives are not as linear as they might seem. The closed shape on the left is reminiscent of the Japanese enso—the circle that is painted roughly by Zen master calligraphers—enclosing the void and yet symbolic of the moment. The two parts traditional in haiku and shown by the dash are repeated in the two almost separate shapes captured in the image.

Some advice for those interested in haiga: use a "thrifty" brush and go for the *kokoro*, the heart of the image being recorded. Try too hard and you miss the mark. Become the object and you can't go wrong.

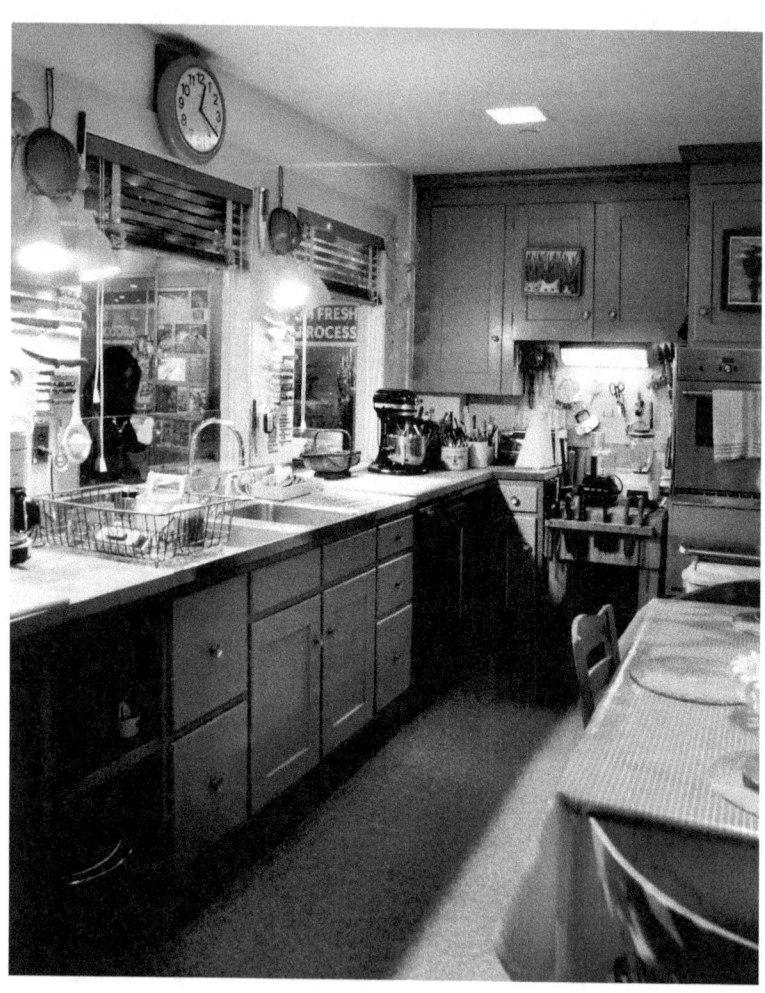

Julia Child's kitchen at the National Museum of
American History (Smithsonian Institution)

the art of
food writing

EVERY YEAR, THE FRIENDS OF THE LIBRARY ON OUR
small island have a book sale to raise funds for bringing in
authors of interest to enhance our already well-cultured island. I
am so ambivalent about these annual sales because I am trying
desperately to downsize my library, and yet I yearn constantly to
expand it. On the day of the sale, I find myself almost at the head
of the line-up, as if I had a panting need for additional books.

Inside, I remind myself of our budget and try for restraint.
I glance casually at all the tables and am just about to depart,
not having chosen a single title, when my eyes descend on a
set of books in a nice little case. Can it be? Yes, it is. It's a set of
Elizabeth David's writings on French and Mediterranean food
and includes her revolutionary books *A Book of Mediterranean
Food* (1950) and *French Country Cooking* (1951).

Like Proust's madeleines that catapulted him back to his
childhood, this set of books sent me spinning back to the
post-war period in England when food was still rationed. Can
you imagine what effect David's books describing French and
Mediterranean foods had on a vulnerable, non-domesticated
teenager who had lived on her mother's wartime cooking that
involved dried eggs and dried milk? Courgettes? Aubergines?
Paella? Moussaka? Ratatouille? Hummus? Gazpacho? What on
earth were they? The sensuality of being lost in the world of, for
me, exotic restaurants and recipes, mixed in with all the sensual
films coming in from the continent after the war years was almost
too much for a slightly inhibited—yet searching—teenager.

As her biographer, Artemis Cooper, said, "David was the best writer on food and drink this country has ever produced. When she began writing in the 1950s, the British scarcely noticed what was on their plates, which was perhaps just as well. Her books and articles persuaded her readers that food was one of life's great pleasures, and that cooking should not be a drudgery but an exciting and creative act. In doing so she inspired a whole generation not only to cook, but to think about food in an entirely different way."

In her own life, David was both frugal and sensible about what constitutes a good meal: "The most elementary hors d'oeuvre such as a plate of red radishes with a few of their green leaves, a dish of green and black olives and another of halved hard-boiled eggs (not overcooked), with butter and bread on the table is ten times more tempting than the same ingredients got up in a pattern all on one dish and garnished with strips of this and dabs of that. You are, after all, preparing a meal, not decorating the village hall."

Elsewhere, she expands this idea: "There are times when one positively craves for something totally unsensational; the meals in which every dish is an attempted or even a successful tour de force are always a bit of a trial." And here's a further example of her not promoting the excessive: "I do not myself think it necessary to keep a large stock of liqueurs for flavoring fruit compotes and salads, or to bring them blazing to the table at every meal. Indeed the habit of flambéing everything from prawns to figs has become so prevalent that one can now scarcely dine out in London without for a considerable part of the meal being hemmed in by sheets of flame." As Raymond Mortimer, the British writer, said, "The food is too rich and so are the customers."

Elizabeth David, when asked whether it was awful to always be criticizing food and never enjoying it, replied, "Well, if a food writer does not exercise his or her critical faculties to a high degree and with a backing of informed experience, he or she is not doing his or her job." She added that she also wrote of the benefits and pleasures of good food, good wine, and good cookery books. She was so decisively and delightfully opinionated: "A bad meal is always expensive." When it comes to food writers, she is still considered one of England's greatest.

They say you have to be knowledgeable about food in order to be a good food writer, but I am not. However, never daunted by a subject I know little about, when I start to write about a new interest, I do some research and then add my naiveté, which often hits on a freshness that may not have occurred to jaded authorities. Lack of knowledge has never inhibited my essay writing. Writing is always a learning process for me. As for food writing, since I no longer travel further than Vancouver and rarely eat out, my food writing has to come from the disasters and triumphs in my own kitchen.

Still, you may wonder what qualifications I might have that would enable me to give advice to budding food writers. It's true that I have little solid experience myself, apart from sixty-six years of cooking for two husbands and two children. My initial cake baking for my first husband was a cake that sat in the solidity of a pudding. However, years later, and many meals under my belt, or rather eaten by myself and others, I can count two efforts on my part to support my being allowed to offer some suggestions about food writing and the production of cookbooks. First, I wrote a book about a year on my island, in which I offered a seasonal recipe for each month. The second effort that qualifies me to at least lay some thoughts down on paper about food writing is a cookbook I have prepared for my husband, Eli, so that his favorite recipes are there for him to make after I'm gone. This cookbook has been adjusted over the years of our marriage, from vegan to macrobiotic to vegetarian to slightly vegetarian (with the inclusion of fish and the occasional chicken or turkey) to now full-blown everything.

At eighty-eight, I have just rewritten Eli's cookbook for the umpteenth time in order to reduce the number of recipes. After all, how many different hors d'oeuvre does one need to make at my age? I no longer have the energy to stuff mushrooms. Each recipe is one of Eli's favorites, and each recipe has no more than six ingredients and takes no more than thirty minutes to prepare.

One of the recipes I provided in my book *A Gabriola Year*

stemmed from my childhood. I was brought up in an almost-assimilated Jewish family, but the one item of ethnic cooking that I still make that is a remnant from my early years is matzo balls for chicken soup. My matzo balls float divinely, and I add a touch of nutmeg, which horrifies most of my more orthodox friends. The gribenes, chopped liver, tzimmes, kugels, and gefilte fish have all gone by the board, but the matzo balls stay firmly entrenched in my recipe book, even though I have to ferry over to Vancouver Island to find the matzo meal.

My daughter's partner, Fred Baker, had parents who ran the famous 2nd Avenue Deli in New York, and Fred insisted I use his mother's recipe for matzo balls because they never sank to the bottom of the soup bowl, a disgrace by any standards. It's the one I have adopted and, as Fred said, "It never fails." In case you too have a memory of matzo balls as one of your childhood comfort foods, here is Fred's Matzo Balls that Don't Sink:

For 8 to 10 balls—A full cup of matzo meal, 4 eggs, 1/4 cup of vegetable oil, 1/4 cup ice-cold water, 1/2 teaspoon of salt, dash of pepper. Thoroughly whip up the 4 eggs, salt, oil, water, and pepper in a bowl. Now, with the same vigorous whipping motion, slowly pour in the matzo meal, and once you have incorporated all of it, keep whipping it to try to fluff it up as much as possible (a minute at least), then cover it with plastic wrap and put it in the fridge for at least twenty minutes. Meanwhile, bring a half-filled, coverable, 4-quart pot of salted (1 tablespoon) water to a brisk simmer, bubbling, but not boiling fiercely. Take the mixture out of the fridge and place it next to the pot. Run cold water over your hands and have a bowl of cold water nearby to rinse your hands in between making each ball. Now, with wet hands, take a good dip of the mixture to make a ball about 1.75–2 inches in diameter and drop it into the bubbling water. The balls should rise to the surface almost immediately. (If they don't, Fred recommended scrapping the mixture and starting again.) Once the balls are at the surface and the boil is nice and slow, cover the pot, and ten minutes later when you uncover it, you'll find they have grown into beautiful, fluffy 3- to 3.5-inch masterpieces. Turn off the heat and let them float on top and cool for a few minutes. Remove them from the pot and add to the chicken soup that you have previously made. You can then reheat the water for the next batch.

Why should one bother to write about food at all? Well, apart from food being a necessity and therefore well worth writing about, I could do no better than quote a passage by the great food writer M. F. K. Fisher: "It seems to me that our three basic needs, for food and security and love, are so mixed and mingled and entwined that we cannot straightly think of one without the others. So it happens that when I write of hunger, I am really writing about love and the hunger for it, and warmth and the love of it and the hunger for it . . . and then the warmth and richness and fine reality of hunger satisfied . . . and it is all one."

Food writing isn't really different in many respects from other writing; if it's not good, it's not good. You have to find your voice. That is, the writing must read as though you have something urgent and interesting to tell the reader. Your voice must be helpful. In the case of food writing, it should be as if you are accompanying the reader to the restaurant or staying with them while they try the recipe. For this, your writing should be clear and accurate. Food writing differs only in that it accentuates the senses—taste first, but also smell, sound (of biting into food, of water boiling), touch, and sight. Descriptions using the senses should be attractive but not overblown. From the senses one can move on to give the background of the recipe, the restaurant, the area from which the food comes, etc. Most of all, you need passion in food writing (or in any writing, come to that), passion to tell why you love the food, the restaurant, the market you are trying to describe.

What do I look for in good food writing? Cookbooks? Food news? Restaurant reviews? Recipes? Let me just consider cookbook writing, as that concerns me most, for even at my age I am still looking for fresh ways to set food on the table. One thing I want in a great cookbook is an introduction to each recipe, explaining its origins and why the dish is so scrumptious. I like chit-chat at the top of the recipe. I enjoy a few tales of the writer's mother's kitchen to set the scene, but if the writer wanders too far from the subject, I may not want to wander with them. I ask for detailed quantities and steps— how big a carrot? how hard should the water be bubbling? The writer should not assume everyone knows how to poach an egg. I like a clean layout of the recipe page with, if possible, a clear photograph of the dish placed exactly opposite the recipe, attractive enough to intrigue me and make me want to try the recipe. If there is no photograph, the writing should be as graphic as possible, so I can visualize the dish. The recipes should be well tested. I hate to fail because of someone else's errors. I love Julia Child's wont to include what could go wrong at each stage of her recipes. I like recipes to be short and uncomplicated and to have familiar ingredients, for I live on an island that doesn't bring in too many exotic food items. I like variations, so if I don't have one ingredient in the cupboard, I can add another, even if the substitution results in a somewhat different dish. I like to know how many people the recipe will serve; cooking for two most of the while, I don't like to have to eat the same dish for more than two meals running, although often it's better at the second eating. I don't like cookbook writers showing off with a mention of truffles (often white truffles) and exotic wines. I don't eat and drink those items every day, and I suspect the average reader doesn't either. As a person who has budgeted tightly most of my life— and a teetotaler—I can't claim extensive knowledge of either white truffles or wine with the right date on the bottle and so am saved from swanking when I do write about food.

As I said, with age, I seem to want simple recipes, those not involving a load of preparation and the buying of exotic ingredients. And, of course, I prefer large type and measurements in cups and teaspoons; I don't have scales. While I like strong opinions in a cookbook writer, I don't

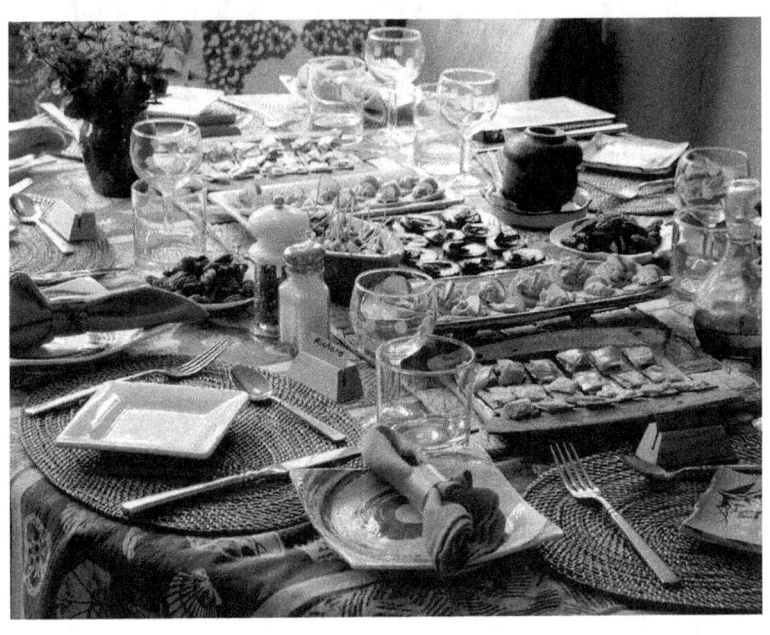

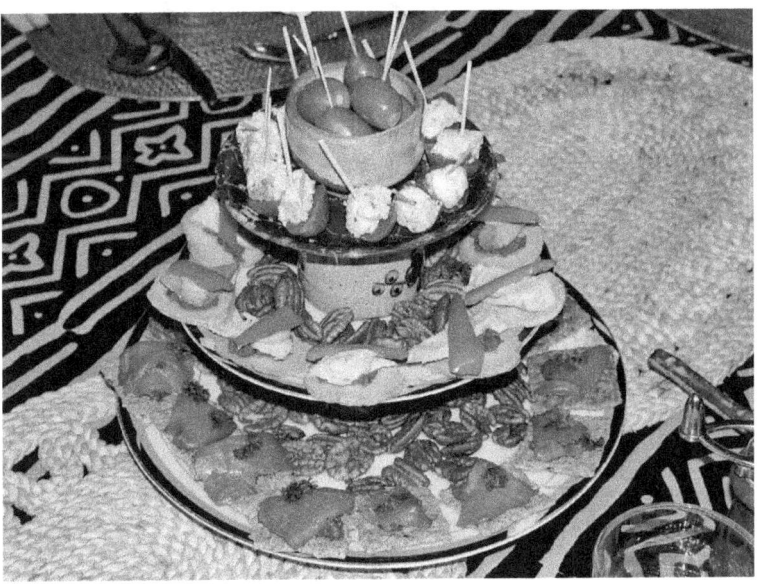

Naomi's presentations of appetizers

like ranting, and I try to remind myself that these are just the writer's opinions, unless they are backed up by solid research.

I believe in re-parenting myself when I start a new project or enter a new stage in life. When I decided to become a full-time poet, I chose Billy Collins as my father and Wisława Szymborska as my mother. For essay writing, I stayed with a single, but very special parent—Montaigne, the father of all essay writers, although, being needy and greedy, I added Phillip Lopate later to keep me au courant.

So who could I suggest as food-writing parents? I did a quick survey. Far and away the most recommended food writer was Irma Rombauer. Her *Joy of Cooking* was my own first bible so many years ago. Other top food and cookbook writers worth studying include Julia Child, Michael Field, Calvin Trillin, M. F. K. Fisher, James Beard, James Villas, Jeffrey Steingarten, Claudia Roden, Tony Bourdain, Ruth Reichl, Ina Garten (The Barefoot Contessa), Michael Pollan, Richard Olney, Marcella Hazan, Craig Claiborne, and Fuchsia Dunlop. Well, that's far too many parents to choose from. Julia Child had enormous influence when, with Simone Beck and Louisette Bertholle, she wrote the 1961 classic *Mastering the Art of French Cooking*. In fact, all Child's food writings are still very popular. Her books *The Way to Cook* and *Baking With Julia,* written with baking author extraordinaire, Dorie Greenspan, rank high. I can't resist commending the United Kingdom's favorite domestic goddess, Nigella Lawson, and the king of vegetable cookery, Yotam Ottolenghi.

In case you are thinking of becoming a professional food writer, please take food critic Phyllis Richman's quote seriously: "[good food writing] is not press trips to Tuscany, not free meals at restaurants, and not the adoration of famous chefs where you sit around saying 'yum, yum' to everything put in front of you."

As I've recently been giving a number of memoir-writing workshops, I am toying with the idea of writing my memoirs in the form of food writing, starting with the cans of Cow and Gate milk that I was fed as a baby and going through the coconut pyramids that were my mother's best cookies, the typical English breakfasts and teas I was served at my residence during my university years, the scientific cooking of my first husband (a chemist and artist), the chocolate ice-cream of my second husband, and so on. In my book of memoirs, *Some Sort of Life*, I almost totally ignored my writing life. I corrected this by devoting an entire book to my life as a poet, *Poetry that Heals*. As cooking and fabric art have also been a big part of my life, devoting memoir books to each of these seems very appealing. Food writers have often used the memoir form for their writing, and I can't recommend enough Ruth Reichl's *Tender at the Bone* and *Comfort Me with Apples*, and M. F. K. Fisher's *The Gastronomical Me*. By the way, if you want a brilliant bit of food writing on the intrigues of the food business, you can hardly beat Nora Ephron's *The Food Establishment*. I love her take on greens: "This was right around the time endive was discovered, which was followed by arugula, which was followed by radicchio, which was followed by frisée, which was followed by the three M's—mesclun, mâche and microgreens—and that, in a nutshell, is the history of the last forty years from the point of view of lettuce."

These days, the web is overloaded with food bloggers, and I know there are far too many cookbooks out there in the world. Yet, even at my age, I'm still looking for that winning piece of food writing, that recipe I just have to try, so I continue to search.

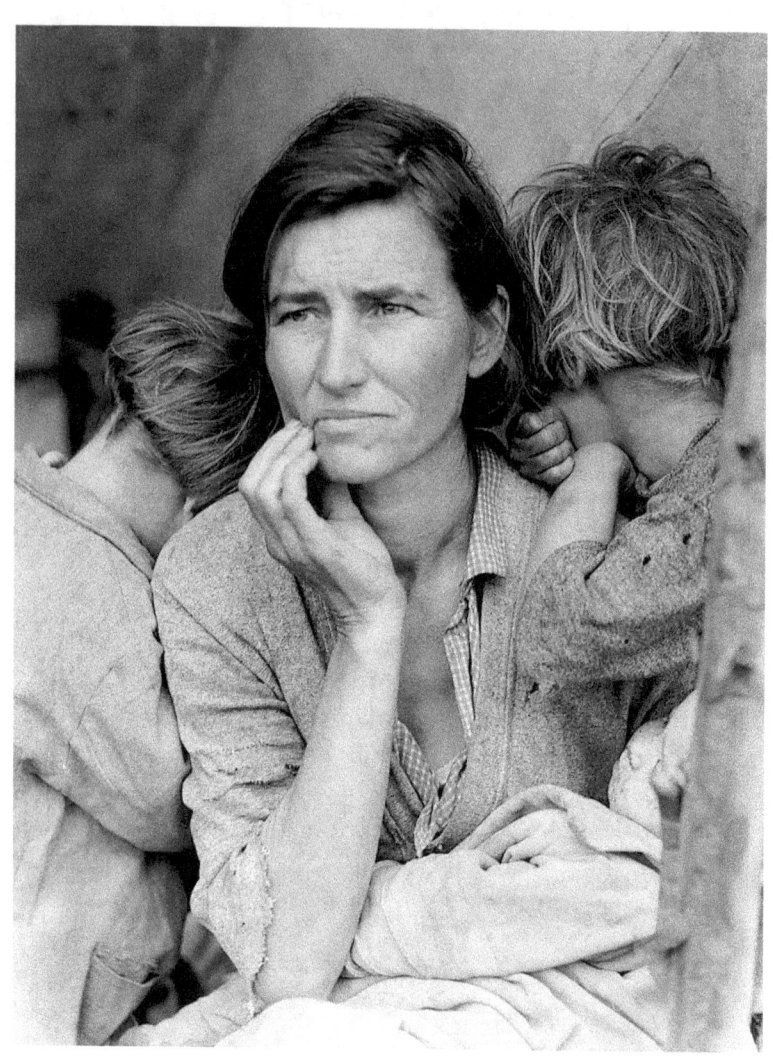

Dorothea Lange, *Migrant Family*

the art of
photography

IN THE SIXTIES, WHEN MY FAMILY WAS YOUNG, AN
outing with my first husband, a chemist/artist/photographer,
would look something like this: he would march ahead carrying
the incredibly heavy Sinar camera in its metal case, I would
follow in his footsteps with the incredibly heavy Manfrotto
tripod, and our two children would drag behind carrying
an assortment of bags holding lenses and filters. These
days, a bright four-year-old can record activities in their pre-
kindergarten class with an iPhone and upload photographs or
videos to the cloud before their parent arrives to pick them up.
Photography nowadays is light and easy, and for these reasons,
the whole world seems to be recording their lives instead of
living them. As Susan Sontag said, "Today everything exists to
end in a photograph." It seems as though photography, which
only fifty years ago was established as a form of "high" art, has
now become an alternate form of reality.

Most people take photos because others take photos; it
is social practice and well embedded as part of family ritual.
Maybe this is to reassure them all that they are somehow
connected, however disconnected they may be in reality; that
they are not breaking apart—in the family album at least;
that they exist and have joined in something together—the
backyard barbeque, the child's first birthday. The photo says,
"These things really happened." Yet, paradoxically, the picture-
taking has invaded the event, made it a little less real because
it is being recorded. On the other hand, press photographers

are guilty of non-intervention as they photograph the horrors of wartime killing or the terror of a street crime, having chosen to record it rather than step in and, at least in some measure, prevent the occasion happening.

Has photography made us more compassionate as we gaze at, say, W. Eugene Smith's famous picture of a mother with her child suffering from Minamata disease? Or has the constant stream of news-disaster pictures gradually made us immune to the suffering of others, as if they were some picture show that will shut down and we will all go home safely?

Regarding travel, photos assure the folks back home that the trip was actually made and that the beauty spots and famous buildings were actually visited. Does taking photographs on a trip make the tourist feel a little less a stranger in a strange land? Does taking photographs make them feel a little less guilty that they are not working while others around them are, or a little less guilty because they are photographing wildlife rather than killing it? Or maybe photography makes us all tourists in others' realities, even our own.

Photographs have opened the whole world to us; barely an area is left unrecorded, hardly a group of people unimaged as we become hooked on the idea that we know something after we have looked at a photograph. But what do we know? That the world is full of suffering? Of delights? Of beauty? Of distortion? Of what have all these images actually informed us when we are photographing reality rather than living it? Or rather, hasn't the photograph become more real than the reality? Is the Taj Mahal a bit of a let-down when we finally walk its paths?

For me, photography is an infinitely sad thing—even if it records great happiness—in that it reminds constantly that this moment being captured will never come again. All is ephemeral, no matter how firmly recorded it may be. Photography is an art of nostalgia.

Early twentieth-century photographs imitated painting in their softness, but when photographers, such as Edward Steichen, started to photograph everyday things, such as a milk bottle, photography became a new way of seeing. The ordinary was made extraordinary when Edward Weston did his series of green pepper photographs, inspiring a generation of black-and-white photographers by showing them that everyday objects could take on sculptural forms of both interest and beauty. As he said, "Anything that excites me for any reason, I will photograph; not searching for unusual subject matter, but making the commonplace unusual."

Photography began to make the whole world democratic, in that things we hadn't given much value to were photographed as of equal import to the photographs of distinguished people, famous buildings, or valuable objects.

As curator of that most famous of photography shows, *The Family of Man* (first shown at the New York Museum of Modern Art in 1955), Steichen described his aim to be to demonstrate that "the art of photography is a dynamic process of giving form to ideas and of explaining man to man. The show was conceived as a mirror of the universal elements and emotions in the everydayness of life—as a mirror of the essential oneness of mankind throughout the world." Critics have called the show a magazine photo collection, a propaganda display for the American Empire of the Fifties, but I see it as a plea to humans to find their mutual humanity. It's true that the photos didn't show the full range of human sexuality and probably showed developing countries in a rather quaint, National Geographic kind of way, but it is wrong to judge a body of work from one time with our moral outlook of today. Of course *The Family of Man* reflected American views at that time; what else could it do? Not only was the show the most widely seen collection of photographs, probably even taking into account later years, but the book that recorded the show subsequently sold over five million copies. Steichen and his staff went through over two million photos in their final selection of 503 from the submissions of just 273 photographers; the works of famous photographers juxtaposed the works of unknowns. Many of the photos in this exhibition, such as Eugene Smith's image of two small children walking together—*The Walk to Paradise Garden*—

and Dorothea Lange's photo of an impoverished farmwife with her children—*Migrant Family* (p. 68)—became well imprinted on the public consciousness for years after. Just a quick look through the book and you will see the works of most of the famous photographers of the first half of the twentieth century—Robert Capa, Henri Cartier-Bresson, Dorothea Lange, Diane Arbus, Bill Brandt, Walker Evans, Margaret Bourke-White, Eugène Atget, Wayne Miller, Werner Bischof, W. Eugene Smith, Alfred Eisentaedt, and Edward Weston, to name just a few.

Seventeen years later, the same museum showed Diane Arbus's photographs, which disturbed with their images of fringe people we don't care to look at. Neither show was complete then, was it? Did Arbus's works draw us together as human beings or alienate us even further apart? The question I am really asking is, perhaps, does photography draw us closer to the truth or take us further away? How does it help us be more human?

All the photographs in *The Family of Man* exhibition were unframed, mounted on board, and all were black-and-white. What is it about black-and-white photographs that draws so many people to them? Black-and-white allows the photographer to more easily identify what he/she wants you to concentrate on. Black-and-white photography, without the distraction of color, lets you clearly see the strong shapes, negative space, forms, and textures in the photographs. Somehow, black-and-white photographs seem closer to defining the photograph as its own particular art form, rather than it merely being a record of touristy "I was there" shots. Color photographs seem to rouse emotions more, it may be true, but black-and-white asks you to go deeper than surface feelings and to sense the true import of the picture. Nostalgia lends itself to a limited palette; black-and-white gives a feeling of timelessness with its mysterious qualities and its elegance. As a viewer, I like a challenge, and color is just too easy. Of course, there are many proponents of black-and-white photography even in this digital age, but here I'd just like to mention a few of those earlier masters.

For black-and-white portraiture, Yousuf Karsh and Richard Avedon come to mind. Avedon established himself with his portraits before he turned to fashion photography. He was originally employed to do photographs for ID cards for merchant marine seamen. "I had probably photographed one hundred thousand baffled faces before I realized I had become a photographer," he said. Avedon's portraits were distinctive because of his trademark white backgrounds, which intensified the portrait by removing everything around it. As Avedon himself wrote, "The white background isolates the subject from itself and permits you to explore the geography of the face; the unexplored continents in the human face." Indeed, in his portraits, every wrinkle takes on the aspects of a gorge, particularly in the faces of the aged that he captured, such as the staggeringly challenging one of Isak Dinesen. By talking to his subjects about penetrating matters, he was able to get more than the usual superficial record of their persons. No color photo of Marilyn Monroe could beat Avedon's black-and-white one showing her loneliness and vulnerability.

Avedon's portraits of famous people—Charlie Chaplin, Marian Anderson, Martha Graham, and Audrey Hepburn, among others—are quite remarkable in the degree of starkness to which the sitter's personality has been exposed. Yet, his photos of the ordinary people of America—the miners, ranchers, farmers, cowboys, oil field workers—show just as much insight; he gave them the same dignity and attention that he gave his more famous subjects. I love his awareness of how much of himself he put into those portraits: "When the sitting is over, I feel kind of embarrassed about what we've shared. It's so intense. Snapshots that have been taken of me working show something I was not aware of at all over and over again I'm holding my own body or my own hands exactly like the person I'm photographing. I never knew I did that, and obviously what I'm doing is trying to feel, actually physically feel, the way he or she feels at the moment I'm photographing them in order to deepen the sense of connection." His portraits are, as curator Helle Crenzien said, "radical and brutal." Certainly, none of his images of celebrities reflect the public image people were used to seeing.

Avedon dislodged his subjects with disturbing questions before the shutter closed, thus his subjects' images seem to query how they have been defined in life before the moment of being photographed. Avedon said of this, "A photographic portrait is a picture of someone who knows he's being photographed and what he does with this knowledge is as much part of the photograph as what he's wearing or how he looks." Avedon's show *In the American West* was germinal in getting photography accepted as "high" art and exhibited in art museums.

Both Avedon and Karsh were masters of black-and-white portraiture. While Avedon went for intimacy and sheer emotional contact, Karsh made his subjects into heroes by using theatrical lighting and careful poses. Karsh aimed to make his subjects (and also his photos of them) reach an archetypal and immortal level. Photography does rather alter the past as it frames and crops and captures the present and puts it in the file marked "history," doesn't it? Karsh's photographs of Hemingway, Einstein, George Bernard Shaw, and, of course, Winston Churchill are unforgettable. Here's Karsh on his "moment" of clicking the shutter: "There is a brief moment when all there is in a man's mind and soul and spirit is reflected through his eyes, his hands, his attitude. This is the moment to record."

For black-and-white landscape photography during this period, Ansel Adams was the declared master. His photos of the American West have influenced photographers from around the world. Adams's lifelong advocacy for preserving nature helped establish and maintain America's national parks. He declared, "Both the grand and the intimate aspects of nature can be revealed in the expressive photograph. Both can stir enduring affirmations and discoveries, and can surely help the spectator in his search for identification with the vast world of natural beauty and wonder surrounding him."

For humanity in photography, nobody beats Dorothea Lange's images of migrant workers. With her stark black-

and-white photographs, she was able to draw the nation's attention to the plight of the unemployed and homeless during the Great Depression. Of her most famous photograph (p. 68), Lange said, "I saw and approached the hungry and desperate mother, as if drawn by a magnet. I do not remember how I explained my presence or my camera to her, but I do remember she asked me no questions. I made five exposures, working closer and closer from the same direction. I did not ask her name or her history. She told me her age, that she was thirty-two. She said that they had been living on frozen vegetables from the surrounding fields, and birds that the children killed. She had just sold the tires from her car to buy food. There she sat in that lean-to tent with her children huddled around her, and seemed to know that my pictures might help her, and so she helped me. There was a sort of equality about it."

Lange's intensity is reflected in her quote: "One should really use the camera as though tomorrow you'd be stricken blind."

For me, black-and-white photographs have a dreamlike quality. The tones, the shades, the shadows are so subtle that they capture your full attention. I like its wabi-sabi quality. Because it could be considered an "old-fashioned" medium, it is so good for recording images of rustic, worn, and simple objects and scenes. In the photographing of aged human beings, wrinkles and creases take on a sculptural interest when caught in black-and-white. I suppose my appreciation of black-and-white photography reflects my pared-down lifestyle, and although Karsh and Avedon photographed the rich and famous, their ability to say what they wanted to say meets my demand for the highest integrity in the image made. Digital photos can be set for black-and-white, but it is the exploration of black-and-white photography by earlier masters that I turn to time and time again when I want solace from the blare of present-day, color-saturated, bombarding images.

And where is beauty in all this? It is true that photography has shown us the beauty in everyday things and has also presented the "disturbing" and "ugly" in photos that can only be called "beautiful" in their truthfulness, but hasn't it also defined beauty for us, so that we all aspire to celebrity beauty, and aim that our homes reflect those in *Architectural Digest* and our gardens those of master gardeners? Have we gained in the balance, or have we made appearances weigh over substance because of the world of images that has overwhelmed our judgment?

Susan Sontag is quoted as saying, "the painter constructs and the photographer discloses," but what do they disclose—their own take on the world or reality as it really is? It is true that photographers have changed the way we see things from the microscopic to the telescopic. Thanks to photography, we look more carefully at the sky, at the soil, at the comings and goings of human beings. We look more intently, but are we just looking for the novel, the exotic, the fashionable, the spectacle that will startle us from our comfort zone, or are we really looking to penetrate the everyday in order to see the magic within?

Does it matter that the photographer's personal view of the world is what is exposed? After all, the poet and painter also filter the world through their conditioning. Ansel Adams felt that "the true expression of what one feels about life in its entirety" marked a great photograph. So maybe Karsh's desire for immortality and Avedon's desire to show faults were ways of telling their truths. In this respect, I love Minor White's quote that landscape photographs are really "inner landscapes." As Ansel Adams insisted, photographers "make" photographs, they don't just "take" them.

Photographs have, by their reproducibility, influenced traditional art. This is reflected in the consumerism of painting these days, where the work is produced by twenty or more anonymous assistants and, when finished, reproduced in infinite numbers. Photographs and works of art have both become consumer objects distanced from the creating hand. No longer belonging to the elite, photography has liberated creative work, and thanks to digitalization, a created image can immediately be in one's hands, on one's computer, and distributed around the world. Moments are made into immediate history, and by morphing of images, even the present can be projected into a suggested future. Among this profusion of images, the dangers of image-making being used for surveillance and political control of the masses seems a very real threat.

But apart from this dangerous use of photography, the ubiquitousness of images troubles me, and I long for the time when images counted, when photographs were hand-developed and looked at in wonder, a time when a photograph could

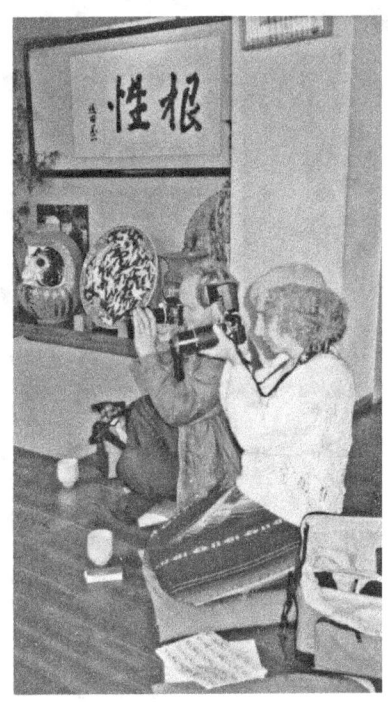

Naomi and Elias photographing at Sadogatake Beya

still our heart or set it beating rapidly, and maybe a time when the clarity of black-and-white photographs extracted all we needed to know from the moment—the times of Atget, Weston, Adams, Evans, and Bourke-White. And the time of Cartier-Bresson, who simply "craved to seize the whole essence in the confines of one single photograph, of some situation that was in the process of unrolling itself before my eyes."

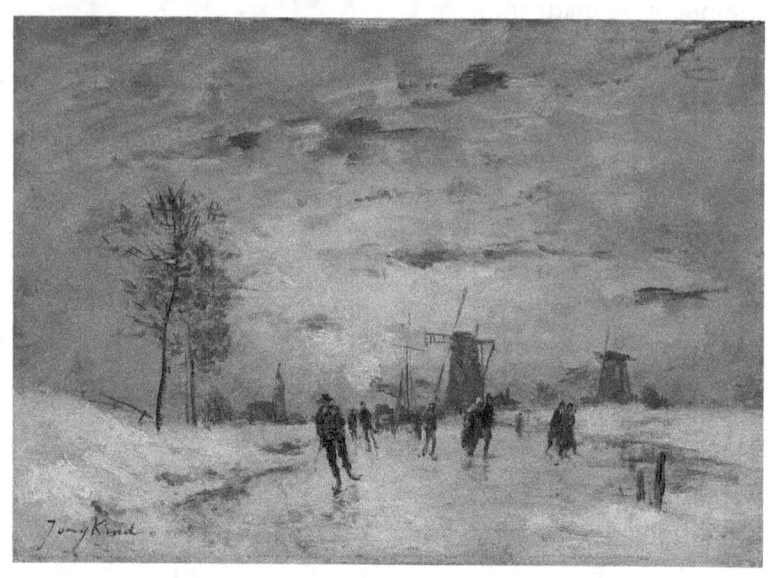

Skating in Holland was attributed to Johan Bartold
Jongkind but is now believed to be a forgery.

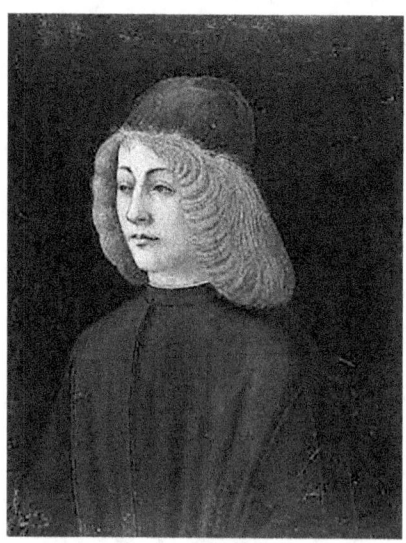

Portrait of a Young Man was attributed to fifteenth-century painter Piero
Pollaiuolo, but is now believed to be a forgery created in the nineteenth century.

the art of
faking

THERE IS A DIFFERENCE BETWEEN HOAX AND FORGERY.
A hoax is a fake that is exposed at a certain time, possibly to
embarrass, often to jolt the person hoaxed out of their rigid
views. A hoax is temporary. A forgery, on the other hand, is
almost never revealed. The hope, I suppose, is that the forgery
will stay hidden until the death of the forger.

When I first got caught up in hoaxes and forgeries, I read
about Tom Keating, who had two thousand of his forgeries
circulating in galleries; Eric Hebborn, who forged to challenge
the art world; Han van Meegeren, who sold six million dollars
worth of fake Vermeers; John Myatt, who sold his fakes
through Christie's and Sotheby's auction houses; and Elmyr
de Hory, who sold a thousand forged paintings to galleries. At
some point, all these forgers—fine artists in their own right—
became jumbled in my mind as to who they copied and why
they did it. When things get so confused, I usually write about
them in the hopes that the words on the page clarify what I
have learned or what I need to say. So I'll start with the basic
forgery problem, which is, as I see it, whether or not a much
admired forged painting is considered a valid piece of art
when it is found out to be fake.

Forgeries, I think, make us uncomfortable. They make us
continually ask why a forgery is not of equal value when it
exactly resembles the original. Most galleries and museums
own forged works of art wrongly attributed to the original
artist. Why, when they are discovered, are they discounted?

It's true that when I am told something is a forgery, I am upset. Even though I can't see any difference between it and the original, I now feel I might see differences in the future if I came to know more about the original artist and looked more closely at the painting. Finding out an object is a forgery immediately changes my attitude to the piece in question.

Forgery is thought to be morally wrong. The forger has misrepresented his/her work, thus damaging the reputation of the artist they have copied and violating the public trust. Failure of trust saddens us, but that is, I think, because we are naive. Forgery is also considered morally wrong because it is a misrepresentation often done for financial gain.

In Western culture, we place a great deal of value on originality. Original only happens once. We claim that originality shows a new aspect of our universe. Originality is esteemed because it changes all subsequent art works in that genre. The original artist is expressing their humanity, therefore it insults us to have a forger present us with a fake. But placing too much value on originality condemns the copy, doesn't it? Why can't the copy be valued for the skill that has gone into it? Copies are not to be despised, for they not only are a way for art students to learn from their predecessors, but could be a record of a lost original, show how one age views another, or be works of art in their own right. Of course, it becomes a forgery when it is attributed to other than the artist who made the copy.

If something in a gallery that has long been admired is declared a forgery, our ideas about the original artist's complete oeuvre might be questioned. Van Meegeren's *The Disciples at Emmaus* was praised by noted art scholar Abraham Bredius (a Vermeer specialist) and hung in the Boijmans Museum for seven years where it was acclaimed by many to be Vermeer's greatest achievement. Van Meegeren's work essentially introduced a whole unknown period in Vermeer's life with his fake Vermeer religious paintings, so at one time we thought Vermeer didn't use the Bible as a source for his paintings, and then we did . . . and then we didn't when the forgery was disclosed.

Forgery is important historically, legally, and financially, but is it wrong aesthetically? If people find the forged work beautiful, then it is beautiful. One collector has said that he had been enjoying them—the forgeries he had purchased unknowingly—for years and would continue doing so.

But, I protest, the original is a personal expression; the forgery is merely an aesthetic object. Forgery is technique with no originality. But is that true? Some forgeries are pastiches of bits from a certain artist's canvases, but some forgeries introduce new elements, and some could be better described as paintings "in the style of" since they are of almost all new subject material and just mimic the artist whose work is being forged. While Eric Hebborn combined elements that might fit in with a known artist—a helmet from one battle scene with the posture of a figure from another painting—Van Meegeren totally invented Vermeer's religious period.

Of course, forgery matters to the purchaser of the fake. I believe that there is nothing illegal about making a fake work of art. It is only when it is labeled and put up for sale as the original that the law steps in. If the purchaser is a museum, then it calls into question their whole collection. Estimates around twenty percent are given for the paintings that are now in museums and galleries that will, in the future, be declared not to be by the artists they are attributed to. Dedicated art lovers will begin to question their trust in art institutions. To the average viewer, though, it may not mean so much.

Often when a painting or sculpture is restored or revarnished, it is nudged back to a supposed brilliant original. This can be a subtle change, or if substantial, could it also be viewed as fake? Philosopher of aesthetics Francis Sparshott has pointed out that the restored Knossos frescoes made the Minoan civilization look Art Nouveau. Restoration is blending with forgery as people want to see bright, pristine-condition paintings and sculpture. Is a well-restored painting the same as the original, or is it a copy?

How do forgers give themselves away, I wonder? Of course, they don't want to, but what are the guilty signs? Everything we do is a display of our individuality, and so it is with the forger. They can't help introducing into the forgery their own mannerisms in the way they make a stroke or draw a line. Because they are copying, forgers will be working more slowly than the original artist, and this will leave tell-tale marks on the canvas. The copier lacks the freedom that originality and spontaneity lend to the execution of a work. Also, a copy lacks the variety of pressures of the original. As the sequence of lines in a copied drawing may not be copied accurately, the rhythm of the original drawing will be lost. All these factors expose the forger, besides the obvious mistake of their often using paper, paint, and canvas from the wrong period.

The forger works within the taste of their time. It is hard to paint in the style of an era not your own. Hebborn thought he could escape this limitation, and maybe he could. Several forgers claim they were "channeling" the artist they were copying. Tom Keating claimed to have channeled Rembrandt, Goya, and Degas. Maybe, because forgers often admire the original artists intensely, they can move into a somewhat similar creative space that overcomes the work looking as though it was made in the present. Of course, if one can enter into the timeless world from which the best artists draw their inspiration, this might be possible.

Hebborn compared himself to a good translator. In his book *The Art Forger's Handbook*, he tells exactly how to make a fake. For example, if you want to forge a signature successfully, view it as abstract lines, i.e., as if it were a drawing. As colors on a new painting blend as they age, therefore making it easy to spot a recent fake, Hebborn advises on what paint, as well as canvas, paper, and frame material to purchase. Obviously, it is easier to fake a recent painter because their materials are still readily available.

What would make a person want to become a forger? It is not always for the money. Sometimes it is because the forger's own artwork is not being accepted by the art establishment, yet they have an urgent need to have their talent recognized, even if they put another artist's name as signature. In the case of Eric Hebborn, forgery was a form of protest at the corruption and distortion of the art world He determined to pass all his fake works past experts. He got loads of prizes himself in his early artistic days; but when it came to his forgery period, he only felt he had succeeded in a forgery when an expert assigned it to the artist Hebborn was copying. As to his reasons for forging, Hebborn felt that the whole art gallery system was unethical and at the mercies of avant-garde fashion as defined by the critics, the curators, and the wealthy collectors—this, at the expense of the impoverished artists. To this end of exposing the system, he left small clues on his forgeries, such as using materials not used in the twentieth century for a twentieth-century copy. After his forged works had passed the experts, he wanted them to be discovered in order to show his contempt for the folks in power in the art world.

Elmyr de Hory gave a good example of a forger's motives when he explained, "My better work I couldn't sell to the galleries at any price. But if I brought them the same drawing with the signature of Picasso, they were ready to peel out any amount of money." De Hory forged over a thousand works of art, mostly those of French masters, and he was successful because he chose a period he understood best—his own period. He actually knew many of the painters he forged. De Hory was a master at portraits and figures, and this was the genre of painting he forged.

Not all forgeries are copies and a copy isn't necessarily a forgery. Historically, student assistants often made copies of their masters' works in the process of their studies. Some masters passed off these copies as their own. Making forgeries was accepted practice at the time because it was treated as payment for tuition.

Copying in art being wrong is such a Western concept. The masters in Bali and Tibet demand their students do exact copies to make the work true to the tradition. These days, the distinctions between copies, reproductions, and deliberate forgeries seem rather blurred.

While Hebborn claims that scientific methods for examining objects of art are in their infancy, such techniques are being developed in leaps and bounds. A few modern dating systems are carbon dating, for dates back to ten thousand years ago; white-lead dating, for dates up to sixteen hundred years ago; and X-ray dating. Underlayers can also be explored with ultraviolet fluorescence and infrared analysis. A most recent development is the statistical analysis of digital images of paintings, which can show if different artists worked on the same painting or whether the painting was done by whomever it is claimed did it.

Museums should be stricter in their accreditation policy and follow the very conservative—and legally safer—attributes given by auction houses. It has been stated that it is the *labeling*, and *only* the *labeling* of a picture that can be false; there is not and never can be a false painting or drawing, or for that matter, any other work of art. Here are the labeling rules the auction houses use:

- If the work is genuine and with perfect provenance, the label states the artist's name as well as birth and death dates. (The poorer the provenance, the more likely the work is to be a fake.)

- "Attributed to the artist" is the phrase used when the auction house is not completely comfortable with the provenance.

- "Studio of the artist" is the phrase used when the work was likely under the supervision of the artist. As assurity declines, other phrases are used, such as "circle of," "style of," or "follower of."

- The phrase "after the artist" is used in cases where the work is assumed to definitely be a copy.

- "School of" is on the label when no particular artist can be attached in any way to the painting.

When selling a painting or drawing these days, the name attached seems to be everything. Art was originally anonymous, done in God's service or in the service of the community. No signatures were to be seen. Then, with the Renaissance, came the cult of the individual artist, and that is when signatures started to count. It should be noted, however, that Old Masters' drawings were rarely signed, as they were usually preparations for a large painting, sculpture, or stained glass window.

Famous forgers' works, when discovered, are now bringing good prices in the art market as their notoriety is bringing them fame. Hebborn pointed out that "a fake by a 'good name' is more acceptable than a genuine work by a relatively minor one." He gives as an example a Willem van de Velde that J. M. W. Turner faked. When, later, both the original and the wrongly ascribed copy sold, the Van de Velde got 65,000 pounds and the Turner 340,000 pounds. One can almost hear Turner's sigh when he declared, "Aesthetics don't count, only the market value."

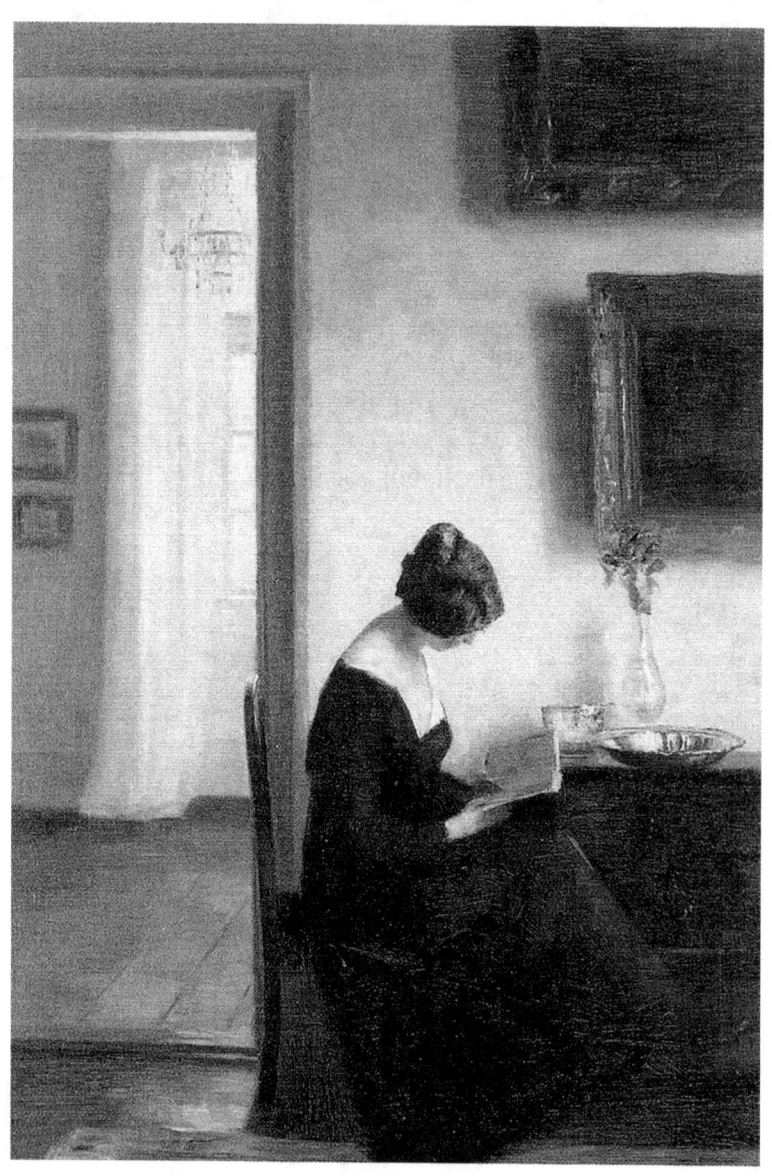

Carl Holsoe, *Woman Reading in an Interior,* early nineteenth century

the art of
reading

WRITER ANDY MILLER SAID THAT "'DEAD-TREE' BOOKS continue their retreat from society, like Napoleon's defeated army of stragglers hobbling away from Moscow to perish in wintry and hostile terrain. Library closures continue apace. Booksellers have gone to the wall in ever greater numbers, chain stores and cozy independents alike; soon the only place to find printed books on the high street may well be charity stores." Still, we read books with paper pages.

Whether you read from an e-book reader or from an old-fashioned paper book, reading is an art, like anything else we do with intensity and concentration. As with all arts, there are techniques that can be adopted in order to read skillfully and optimally.

I think examining why we read is a helpful place to begin. Reading, I feel, gives a book a longer life span, if not immortality. That is, reading extends the writer's purpose to some extent. Besides informing and entertaining, books remind us of things that we already knew but had forgotten we knew. Reading reinforces our ideas and opinions. Reading informs us how others have changed themselves, their neighborhoods, regions, and, in some rare cases, the world. Reading encourages social change, which starts by improving our understanding of ourselves, and reading often gives us the necessary tools to do this. Of course, literacy itself is one of the elements that brings about change.

Reading suggests options and alternatives to help solve

real-life problems. Reading, if properly done, helps us raise questions, and questions are always a good beginning for change. The experience the writer is sharing can reflect our own, and so knowing we are not alone can be a solace in difficult times.

Reading offers new ways of viewing the world, which might release us from too narrow a point of view. It can take us beyond our own experience of life, for it can introduce other cultures, other lifestyles, other ways of behaving. This knowledge can only enrich the reader, for after you've finished reading a book, you should feel changed and rewarded. You should feel you understand human nature a little better because you've lived the lives of a variety of characters and they have given you fresh ideas. Therefore, you can be open and empathetic to a wider range of people. Reading should take the reader on a journey they have not taken before.

Of course, reading can also be cathartic. Reading can stir up feelings we haven't been in touch with recently, and I'm assuming it might be good to get in touch with them, for laughing and crying are both good for releasing tense body muscles.

Reading doesn't have to always be so earnest; it can just be for escape. As Somerset Maugham said, "To acquire the habit of reading is to form for yourself a defense against most of the ills of life." He adds, "All literature is escapist."

And yes, you should want to re-read the book—immediately, or certainly later—that is, if the book had any impact on you worth noting. And speaking of noting, Nabakov said the obvious, "The perfect reader is one who reads with a dictionary and a pencil."

Whether you skim or deep read slowly, it is you, the reader, who makes the book complete by extracting the best you can from it. In a way, you recreate the book when you read it well. The reader is as important as the writer, for without the reader to draw out meaning from the text, the text just sits on the page as a pile of squiggles. The reader gives it life. We interpret the text, comment on it, agree, disagree, associate it with other things we have read or been taught . . . oh, reading is a complex thing!

Readers have a serious responsibility. The writer provides the stimulus, but it is you, the reader, who joins the dots, expands and extrapolates to make of the text what you will. Whether you give the book your full attention or dip and bob to extract your need of the moment, the writer requires you, the reader, to make the work complete. Reading is an act of translation, the reader guessing the essence of the words, adding to it his or her own interpretation, which depends on factors such as cultural background, conditioning, and genetic inclination. As Alberto Manguel put it so nicely: "imbuing the text with the circumstances of the reader."

Writers, I feel, read differently. I, myself, read with a ferocity and laser concentration that surprises even me. At the same time, my mind seems to drift off in schizoid fashion. I know this sounds impossible, but it's the best description that I can give of the process. This way of reading causes me to have thoughts about the text while at the same time, entirely fresh ideas come into my head—unusual connections and linkages that present new insights—often entirely way off the topic I am reading about. My reading complements and enriches my writing. When I read, I continually edit, reading on critical alert. When I find some marvelous writing, I take time to examine carefully how it has been pulled off. As a writer, I pick up on the striking use of a word, the odd phrase that hits me as apt, the brilliant idea, the startling image; and I let them weave this way and that in my mind. If, by chance, a poem or an idea for an essay comes from all this paradoxically almost passive activity, then I feel the book has enriched me, and I have enriched the author by taking the ball he/she has thrown and run with it. Do not mistake this process for plagiarism, although writers do tend to read as predators, seeking stimulus for ideas. Alberto Manguel described this as, "like pelicans regurgitating for the benefit of others."

When I read a book, I might, to enrich the experience, read other books by the same author, read the author's autobiography (if they have done one), and any biographies written on him or her. This gives me a more solid feel for the author's background, their development, and their approach to writing and to life.

Readers in early times read out loud. It was thought necessary to share the decoded page with others, some of whom perhaps couldn't read. Reading silently was considered very strange. Apparently, it was not until the tenth century that people began to read silently as a normal process. Reading silently allows concentrated thought, for when one reads aloud, someone might interrupt with questions or comments. But some say that reading silently encourages daydreaming. Reading silently, admittedly, doesn't allow for any but the reader to censor the writer—"unwitnessed communication," as Alberto Manguel put it.

If we read speedily and without empathy, we remain an outsider to what the book can offer. People read on average 200-250 words a minute, and a good reader is five times faster. If you speed-read, that may be enough for what you need to get from a book. I read very fast, and this aggravates my husband who is a slow, intense reader. Once, as I was reading a book on popular physics, he challenged me to tell him, after reading a chapter, what the chapter had been about. I accepted—for one chapter only—and came off with at least colors, even though they may not have been flying very high.

I wonder how many people read the introduction, preface, dedication, footnotes, end notes, and appendices of a book. Samuel Johnson, of dictionary fame, read in very uneven ways, often skipping around and leaving pages uncut. He said, "I do not suppose that what is in the pages that are closed is worse than what is in the pages that are open." (Pages of books are assembled by folding large sheets of paper that have been printed on. Prior to the mid-nineteenth century, books were sold without trimming the pages to open the folds, thus were "uncut.")

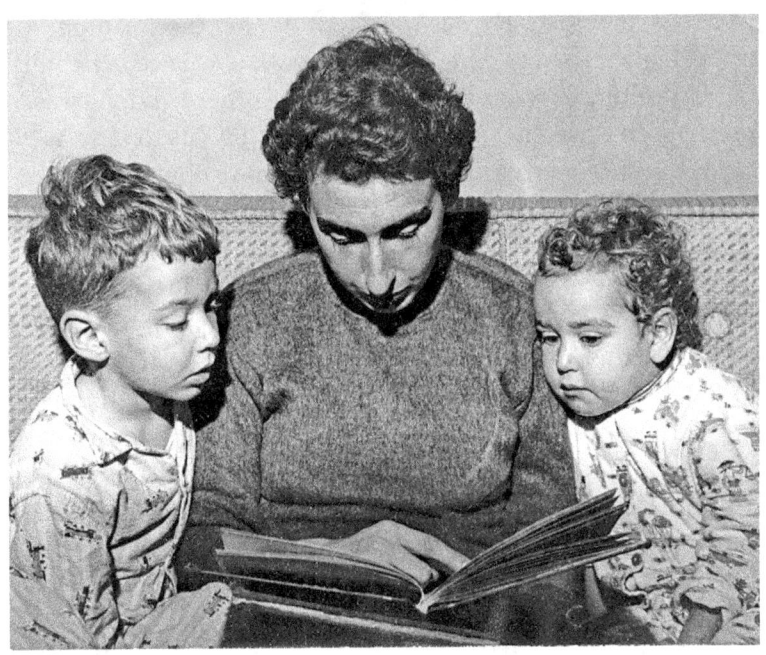

Naomi reading to her children

Reading with Google as an assistant is truly an amazing experience. As you read, for example, a Victorian biography, you can immediately see letters in the subject's own handwriting on the screen. Google, in a flash, provides the images and annotations that augment the text you are reading.

For me, one book leads to another as naturally as events follow each other in life; only rarely does a U-turn happen. The order in which we choose to read books is interesting. Reading one book after a certain other book might affect the way we feel about the previous book. Alberto Manguel's *The Library at Night* threw all other books I had read about libraries into the shadows. Had I read it first, I might never have bothered reading the others, for it was so fine and all-encompassing.

Though he knew little of the functioning of the brain, Socrates fretted that reading, being a solitary art, would not provide the depth of question and understanding that discourse provided. He was right to worry because reading, not being wired in us when we are born, is a learned capability that definitely re-wires the brain. On the other hand, he was not right to worry, because reading also allows us to raise as many questions as discourse does, though we do not get a response from the page.

As Socrates worried, so today's educators are also worrying as young brains are re-wiring to deal with immediate digital information, obtained seemingly without any effort on their part. Professor Maryanne Wolf, Director of Reading and Language Research at Tufts University, in her book on the story and science of the reading brain, *Proust and the Squid*, is concerned about whether "our children are learning the heart of the text of the reading process: going beyond the text." She is with historian Edward Tenner who asks whether Google promotes a form of information illiteracy and whether there might be unintended negative consequences of such a mode of learning. "It would be a shame," he is quoted as saying, "if brilliant technology were to end up threatening the kind of intellect that produced it." How will we be reading thirty years from now, and will our re-wired brains be adding qualities to our reading that reading enchanting, old-fashioned books with our old-fashioned brains cannot provide? I wonder.

For those of you who have trouble remembering the contents of books you have read, or even the titles and authors (as I sometimes do), here are a few things I do to help me retain at least something of the book I am reading; perhaps they will help you also. It's natural to remember books that have stunned you far better than books that have been just so-so. This seems obvious, and yet even with some books that seem to have turned me around, I find, a few months after reading them, that certain details just evade me. For that reason, when I read, I tag the pages where interesting ideas or apt quotes appear, and after I have finished the book, I copy these down into a computer file. Reading books out loud, particularly poetry books, somehow reinforces their contents in our brain. If the problem with retention is poor concentration in the first place, perhaps you are not really interested in the book, or perhaps hunger, fatigue, or worry are distracting you. If you really need to retain the information in a book, reading at your time of peak alertness is best. If you are reading for relaxation or escape, then the time you choose is not so important. Reading in an upright position seems, for me at least, to sharpen my attention, although I love to read horizontally, banana-shaped on a couch. This can, however, lead to dozing off.

Because my memory is so bad, I often find myself re-ordering a book from the library that I didn't even want to read the first time. Sometimes I find myself starting to read a book and getting twenty pages into it before it rings a bell, and I realize I'd read it previously. So I now record titles I have read and often make a note about each book.

And when you've finished a book, what do you do with it? If we do not share with others the knowledge we have learned from a book, we are not helping prolong the life of the book. Do you press it on your friends, return it to the library, put it away on the bookshelf? I'll bet my bottom dollar that you don't record it as I have suggested above. When I was younger, book diaries could be found at stationery stores, and I still remember a few of my entries from that time. If you don't record a book, how will you know the details when you wish to recommend or warn against reading it? How will you know what you have read when, maybe years later, you vaguely remember a word in the title and long to read that book again? Place sticky notes on those pages that carry striking thoughts. If it's your own book, you can leave them there for future reference. I have several books that are really important to me sprouting a yellow garden of tabs from the tops of the pages. Being aware that the book you are reading might change you in ways you don't know, why not give the reading process your all?

Montaigne said about his reading habits, "I leaf through books, I do not study them. What I retain of them is

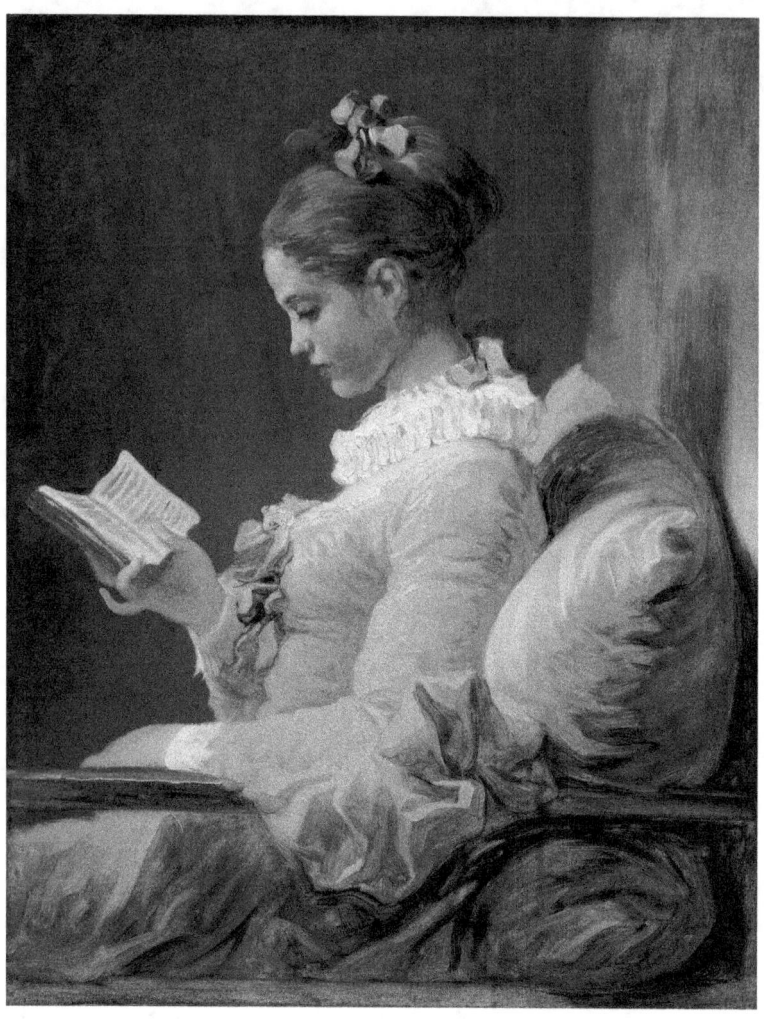

Jean-Honoré Fragonard, *A Young Girl Reading*, c.1770

something I no longer recognize as anyone else's. It is only the material from which my judgment has profited, and the thoughts and ideas with which it has been imbued; the author, the place, the words, the circumstances, I immediately forget."

Yes, the moment one finishes a book, it becomes a summary, a memory; and our memories have less and less relevance to the actual book just read. Our memory of a book once read bears so little resemblance to the original text that one must wonder what we should call the book we are remembering. Somehow, we have rebuilt the book in our own image; the elements that remain are the ones important to us, the rest of the structure might as well have gone to demolition, as Montaigne suggested it should.

If we forget so much when we read, how does reading affect us at all? You must know the answer to this, for when you have read a book that stirs you emotionally or intellectually, at the moment of closing the book, you feel different. You may not consciously analyze in what way you feel different, but the feeling is there nevertheless. However, the question still remains, "What happens to our reading that we can't remember?" Does the brain retain the useful parts of a book, useful to our ego maintenance or to our survival in good physical or mental shape, and does it then cast the rest of the book off in the dross of dreams? And if we only retain a small part of our reading that we seem to consciously need, does that drive us to continue reading as we search for bits of ourselves that we have neglected or perhaps never even developed?

And then there is re-reading. Reading a wonderful book for the first time is terrible because you can never have that feeling again. Can we read a book a second time and keep Browning's "first fine careless rapture?" I have a shelf of favorites that I can read innumerable times and they never let me down. They include: *The Remains of the Day*, by Kazuo Ishiguro; *Pride and Prejudice*, by Jane Austen; *How to Talk About Books You Haven't Read*, by Pierre Bayard; *84, Charing Cross Road*, by Helene Hanff; *The Curious Incident of the Dog in the Night-time*, by Mark Haddon; *Greengage Summer*, by Rumer Godden . . .

Well, it's quite a long shelf, but every time I re-read these books, I find something new. I know the text stays the same, but I seem to be able to add more to it or perhaps am more prepared to look deeper into it. Is it possible that I have matured between the first and second readings and that all the books I have read in between somehow helped the process?

l'autre, d'vn melange fi vniuerfel, qu'elles effacét, & ne retrouuent plus la couture qui les à iointes. Si on me preffe de dire pourquoy ie l'aymois, ie fens que cela ne fe peut exprimer, fi y a à ce femble au delà de tout mô difcours, & de ce que i'en puis dire, ne fçay qu'elle force diuine & fatale mediatrice de cette vnion. Ce n'eft pas vne particuliere confideration, ny deux, ny trois, ny quatre, ny mille : c'eft ie ne fçay quelle quinte effence de tout ce meflange, qui ayant faifi toute ma volonté, l'amena fe plonger & fe perdre dans la fienne. Ie dis perdre à la verité, ne luy referuant rien qui luy fut propre, ny qui fut ou fien. Quand Lælius en prefence des Côfuls Romains, lefquels apres la condemnation de Tiberius Gracchus, pourfuiuoyét tous ceux, qui auoyent efté de fon intelligéce, vint à f'enquerir de Caius Blofius (qui eftoit le principal de fes amis) côbien il eut voulu faire pour luy, & qu'il eut refpondu, toutes chofes. Comment toutes chofes, fuiuit-il, & quoy f'il t'eut commandé de mettre le feu en nos temples? Il ne me l'eut iamais commandé, replica Blofius. Mais f'il l'eut fait? adiouta Lælius: I'y euffe obey, refpondit-il. S'il eftoit fi parfaictement amy de Gracchus, comme difent les hiftoires, il n'au oit que faire d'offenfer les confuls par cette derniere & hardie confeffion, & ne fe deuoit départir de l'affeurance qu'il auoit de la volonté de Gracchus, de laquelle il fe pouuoit refpondre, côme de la fienne. Mais toutefois ceux, qui accufent cette refponce comme feditieufe, n'entendent pas bien ce myftere, & ne prefuppofent pas comme il eft, qu'il tenoit la volonté de Gracchus en fa manche, & par puiffance & par connoiffance, & qu'ainfi fa refpôce ne fonne nô plus que feroit la miéne, à qui f'équerroit à moy de cette façon: fi voftre volonté vous commâdoit de tuer voftre fille, la tueriez vous? & que ie l'accordaffe, Car cela ne porte aucû tefmoignage de confentemét à ce faire, par Ce que ie ne fuis point en doute de ma volôté, & tout auffi peu

A page of the famous *L'exemplaire de Bordeaux*, a copy of the second edition of the *Essais* with Montaigne's corrections, annotations, and additions for the third (final) edition. This page is from *Essai no. 27* of the first book, entitled "De l'amitié" ("On friendship").

the art of
personal essay writing

THE YOUNGER GENERATION MAY NOT BE AWARE OF THIS fact, but the personal essay did not start with blogging. Michel de Montaigne lived in the sixteenth century and has been, while not my first, certainly my most consistent model for personal essay writing. Other writers who have helped me shape my essay writing have been Charles Lamb, and of more recent vintage, Phillip Lopate, Nora Ephron, Edward Hoagland, David Wallace, Cynthia Ozick, David Sedaris, David Rakoff, Augusten Burroughs, and Sloane Crosley.

It was Charles Lamb's essays, along with Addison's and Steele's pieces for *The Spectator*, studied at school, that first got me interested in small, charming bits of writing that didn't seem demanding and yet held a load of interesting ideas. It was many years later that I met up with the father of personal essayists, Montaigne, and his many-times-descended taker-on-of-the-cloak-of-personal-essayist model, Phillip Lopate, who convinced me, when I wasn't writing poetry, to use the personal essay to express what I wanted to say. Oddly enough, James Burke, while a science essayist rather than a personal essayist, also had an enormous effect on my writing. I loved his *Connections*, where he starts with a subject and moves through a dozen others to make his point. His segues are amazing and one finds oneself, at the end of one of his essays, far from the starting point and yet somehow strangely linked to it. After Burke, segues became my forte.

The online personal essay boom known as blogging—really

a messy mixture of diary, letter, and essay—does seem to be swamping the world. It is certainly the fastest way to gain attention, if that is the writer's aim, and checking the number of "like" and "dislike" clicks they receive every day can become an obsession. Blogging often becomes oversharing; the constant overexposure of the writer's life and their self-confessions is so dominant that they all seem to blur into a pathetic image of the human condition. If blogs had political or social reform in mind, or even personal reform, the thousands of available blogs might be of some use. As it is, I long for the sharp political and personal insights of Nora Ephron, or Phillip Lopate's elegant essays on anything that takes his fancy.

The personal essay has never been granted the full cultural import of the novel, or even the short story. Is it because personal essays are usually so conversational that they often spill over, as blogs do, into self-absorption and the over-confessional? The inner life and passing thoughts and sharp impressions of a fine personal essayist are absorbing because they teach me so much about humankind and the world that I need to know, and they do so in such a seemingly effortless way.

The two most important things to remember, I feel, for folks starting off as personal essayists are: first, start by stating what subject has been chosen, and then offer reflections on it, thinking in public, as it were. The reflecting comments should guard your subject from being too personal, too narcissistic, making your essay more one that can reach out to the reader in a shared humanity. The best personal essays are not sensational, but weave the eternal into the everyday moments recorded.

In order to offer interesting comments on the subject you are writing about, you may have to stray a bit from your main topic. But if this opens it away from a didactic, boring presentation—if it is a fruitful wandering—then that is all to the good. You need to show your reader a fresh and ambivalent mind. This can only happen if you are curious about what you are exploring. If it is a repetition, a rehash of your old ideas, you will be bored and so will your readers. Genuine curiosity on your part will overcome the incessant, narcissistic "I" that you will be using. Your exploration of the subject will have an authenticity that everyone can share. Curiosity plus your own voice will make for winning essays.

As to your own voice, which is the second most important thing to consider in personal essay writing, you should not be writing from self-aggrandizement, nor from self-hatred, but from a middle position where your interesting aspects are shown along with your warts. Modest egotism is enough. While self-aggrandizing is distasteful, masochistic self-putdowns are disenchanting. The art of self-putdown only succeeds if the writer has a fair estimate of their own worth and is using the technique to relax the reader. Sharing your flaws can help the reader feel less isolated as they possibly identify with some of them. Best to show yourself as the complex human being we all are. We are rarely perfectly nice or perfectly horrible. If you don't show your vulnerability in your essays, you won't touch anybody. Be generous of yourself. You need to set up an intimate room where you can tell the reader what you want to say in an afternoon chat over tea and cucumber sandwiches (in my case) or over drinks (about which I know little).

You also need to draw a picture of yourself that will attract the reader, a kind of branding. You are, by writing personal essays, recreating yourself. This doesn't mean you have to present an exaggerated or caricatured you, but it does mean that the "I" you continually use should be provided with background and fleshed out so the reader knows where you are coming from. Set the stage for them. Your quirks, your conditioning, and your life's journey make you a unique person. And for yourself, creating this persona allows you a little distance from whatever you are examining, and that distance is the one that leaves space for presenting the pluses and minuses of your topic.

As far as my persona goes, for a long while I was known as "that lovely old biddy from Gabriola." The title got attached to me in this way. I was having a print job done in Nanaimo, the closest town on Vancouver Island to our little island of Gabriola. They didn't have the machines to do it in Nanaimo, so the printer had to forward the job to a printer in Victoria. In his message to the Victoria printer, the Nanaimo printer started by saying, "I have this lovely old biddy from Gabriola . . ." By mistake, the message came to me. My publisher eagerly adopted it, for one needs branding these days to sell books, and this was, in an odd way, an attractive branding. Of course, when I became Poet Laureate of Nanaimo, my branding was raised a notch or two, I must admit.

Our present society is all for tolerance, as am I, but a few strong judgmental remarks in your personal essays, while they may startle, may also be welcome. Writing that cuts through the crap from time to time is a breath of fresh air among cliché-ridden efforts that try to please and appease. Don't rant or opinionate on purpose though, for it will show. Opinions have to come from a level of genuineness. The reader can be both surprised and intrigued by your questioning of accepted truths, but you have to be prepared to explore your contrarian position, to supply reasons for it. Don't get lost in your point of view, but present it with the scrutiny and the doubt it deserves. As has been said, the personal essay is an example of someone thinking against himself or herself.

Presenting oneself as a curmudgeon, as did Robertson Davies, only works when you actually are one, as he was. Curmudgeon or not, if you don't have opinions and ideas of your own, why should anyone read you? Don't worry if you find that you are contradicting yourself; Montaigne often did. I believe a mature person can hold two opposing views at the same time, each being a partial truth. The essay doesn't need to be balanced; a little lopsidedness attracts.

Phillip Lopate, my present model for personal essay writing, is quoted as saying that "There is more life in the language of prose than just Twitter's 140 characters and Facebook's emoticons." Of course, as the firm promoter of lengthy personal essays, he is prejudiced. Still, a personal essay does have more shape than a journal and more discipline than what is, more often than not, uncontrolled outpouring in blogs. I should modify that comment by noting that as magazines fold in profusion these days, some fine essayists have turned their efforts to blogging as an outlet.

A personal essay does not have the same structure as a work of fiction, even though it is a "constructed" truth. You are selecting aspects of your experience that affect you, so all you can do is present "your truth" and the way you feel about things—your take on the world outside and your take on your own motivations. Your selection of information about an incident is, to some extent, a fiction, for you are bound to have filled in the gaps in your memory with your imagination.

Family and friends may be your main source for your material. I should warn, however, that while preying on one's family might be allowable (take David Sedaris, for example), it doesn't do to continually beat them up. When it comes to writing so close to home, I ask myself: Are we really responsible for others being upset at what we have written about them? How can we know what will cause offence and what won't? If we want to be safe by running the material before the person involved, aren't we selling ourselves short by allowing others to censor our writing? Still, it's good advice, I think, not to use your personal essay to settle scores, and best to have loads of friends so if you lose some it doesn't matter; also make sure you have a good lawyer. Do you really want to write essays that offend no one?

I also demand from my own writing that I surprise myself from time to time, lest I get bored with milking my family and small island for interesting topics to write about. Often, a writer, when they are in flow, will bring out all kinds of wise statements that they weren't aware they held.

And, after a while, when your friends and family may have dried up as sources for provocative essays, it is then that you may have to do some actual research for topics less readily at hand. I find that researching a topic I know little about expands me, not just by providing me new information, but by opening me to a whole section of people whose interests lie in that field. For a subject I know little about, I've found it's best to start with a small aspect of it, lest the enormity of the task I have undertaken overwhelms me. It is alright not to tackle every angle of a topic, for readers should be left feeling they would like to continue the search themselves.

How do you know when your essay is finished? It may be when you suddenly find you have wandered so far from your topic that you don't know how to get back. If you started the essay by declaring your position, the reader will be more likely to follow you through the maze in order to make your point and will forgive you your wanderings. More likely, you will know the end is approaching because your energy will have lagged, maybe even expired, and when it does, it is time to end the essay, for the reader will have likewise felt it was time to draw it to a close.

Now, more on those recent personal essayists who have turned my writing around. Nora Ephron I've discovered rather late in my writing career, but she is my flavor of the month. Here's a quote of hers that I, as an obsessional reader, appreciate, "Reading is escape, and the opposite of escape; it's a way to make contact with reality after a day of making things up, and it's a way of making contact with someone else's imagination after a day that's all too real." Ephron was a star in whatever field she entered, but she was most wonderful in her food, political, and personal essays. Try her *The Story of My Life in 3,500 Words or Less*, but better still, get *The Most of Nora Ephron* and wallow in her sharp, witty, and astute writing. She is funny, without being oppressively and constantly funny like David Sedaris and Sloane Crosley, though they are both marvelous in their own ways. If you are excruciatingly funny, as they are, that's what people expect you to be and trust you will stay in that state forever, which certainly curbs a writer's development.

Other personal essayists I find noteworthy are: Joan Didion—read her thoughtful account of her years in New York in her essay "Goodbye to All That"; E. B. White—has there ever been a better nostalgia essay written than his "Once More to the Lake"?; David Foster Wallace—although he is a serious essayist, for belly laughs read his account of a state fair to end all state fairs in "Ticket to the Fair"; Annie Dillard—starting with her staggeringly wonderfully worded "Total Eclipse"; and David Rakoff—the master of self-deprecatory comments who makes even as well-whipped a subject as plastic surgery entrancingly funny in his essay "Whatsizface"; Rakoff can also tell of things touchingly sad as in "Stiff as a Board, Light as a Feather", his account of his disabled left arm. For a moving personal essay, try John Jeremiah Sullivan's account of an aged author dying, "Mr. Lytle: An Essay." Well, there must be at least another thousand I could add to my "very favorite" list, culled from years of reading and admiring other personal essayists.

After I reread some of these wonderful personal essayists, I take my usual vow to never write another word again. My usual vow, that, as usual, I never keep, for the personal essay is my favorite way of interfacing with the world and also my favorite way of interfacing with myself.

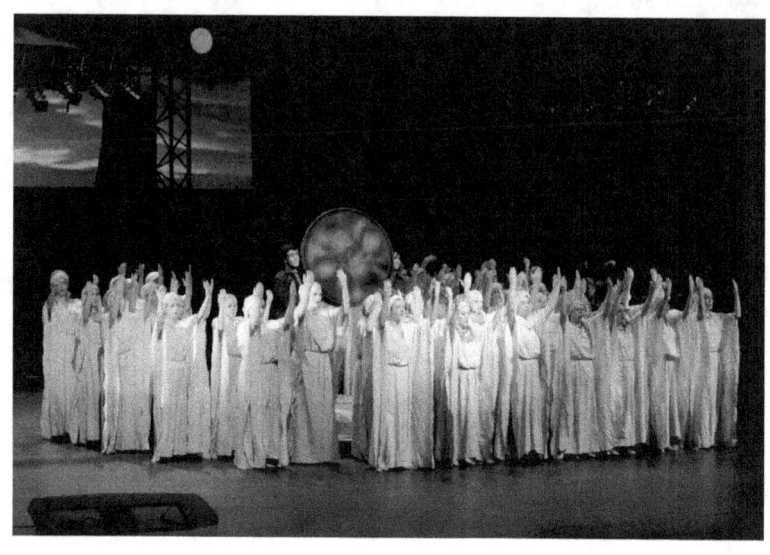

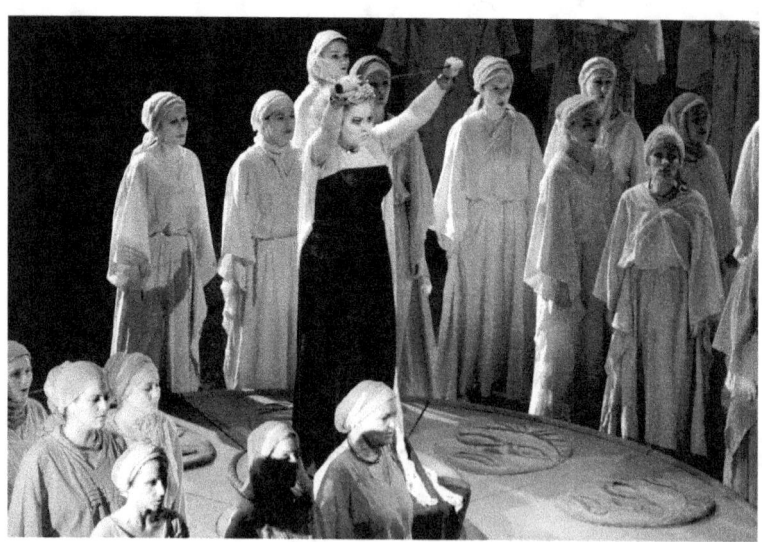

Two scenes from *Norma* by Vincenzo Bellini, performed
by the Serbian National Theatre, 2006

the art of
bel canto

THE NIGHT JOHN F. KENNEDY WAS SHOT, I WENT TO A
Joan Sutherland recital. It was the first time I had seen her in
the flesh, having only listened to her before on radio broadcasts
of the Metropolitan Opera. In the flesh, well . . . she had a
lot of it and was rather gawky. She also had an extraordinarily
large chin. I kept my eyes closed during the performance. As
Dame Edith Evans said, "One of God's pranks was to make Joan
an overgrown schoolgirl and then give her a divine voice." But
when, that evening, Joan sang bel canto excerpts from operas,
especially the ones where the heroine goes mad, the audience
also went mad. At the end of the recital, I, too, found myself
standing with the rest of the audience and waving my program
and calling out "Encore, Encore" with the best of them.

The repertoire for bel canto, or "beautiful singing," consists
mainly of the operas of Bellini, Donizetti, and Rossini written
from the mid-seventeenth century to the early nineteenth
century. The actual term "bel canto," meaning "beautiful
singing," wasn't coined until later. Maria Callas revived bel
canto operas in the early 1950s. Montserrat Caballé said that
Callas "opened a new door for us, for all the singers in the
world, a door that had been closed. Behind it was sleeping
not only great music but great ideas of interpretation." It was
Joan Sutherland, however, who solidified the revival with her
amazing bel canto singing.

Joan Sutherland started off as a mezzo-soprano; it was her
husband, the conductor Richard Bonynge, who pushed her

voice to the place it was meant to go—coloratura soprano. Her tumbling cadenzas could bring tears to my eyes. She could trill on high C, and each note would be heard separately.

From 1956 to the 1970s, I listened to the Metropolitan Opera broadcasts via CBC almost every Saturday. Sometimes I used the interval interview time to drop off my offspring at the skating rink, or wherever they needed to go on Saturday afternoons. But most Saturdays I was glued to the radio, listening for bel canto.

It was during my period of motherhood that bel canto became almost an obsession with me. The operas of Bellini and others were such a lyrical pleasure to hear, contrasting with the vigorous and strident Wagnerian efforts. In fact, Wagner developed his style as a counter to bel canto. I was prejudiced against Wagnerian opera from my baby carriage since my vaguely Jewish parents had banned it from the house because of its association with Nazism and anti-Semitism. My father, also an opera fan, played Enrico Caruso endlessly on our wind-up Victrola, and his favorite opera selection was the quartet from Rigoletto, "Bella figlia dell'amore," sung by Amelita Galli-Curci, Caruso, Flora Perini, and Giuseppe De Luca. To this day, I can see him leaning toward our ornate Victrola cabinet in order to catch their voices.

In the 1950s, it was Maria Callas, Beverly Sills, Joan Sutherland, and Marilyn Horne who did those wonderful bel canto cadenzas with their amazing embellishments and smooth runs from one register to another. Bel canto is incredibly difficult to sing as its long endless phrases have to be carried smoothly and limpidly. I must admit the hitting of high C, as is often required in bel canto, does begin to seem like a circus stunt, as, for example, when Juan Diego Flórez sings Tonio's repeated high C's in Donizetti's *La fille du régiment*. The audience, as if watching a high-wire act, waits for him to miss.

My favorite from this era of bel canto revival is the duet "Mira, o Norma" from *Norma*, sung by Joan Sutherland and Marilyn Horne. I just listened to it again recently and wondered whether the hearing of two female voices

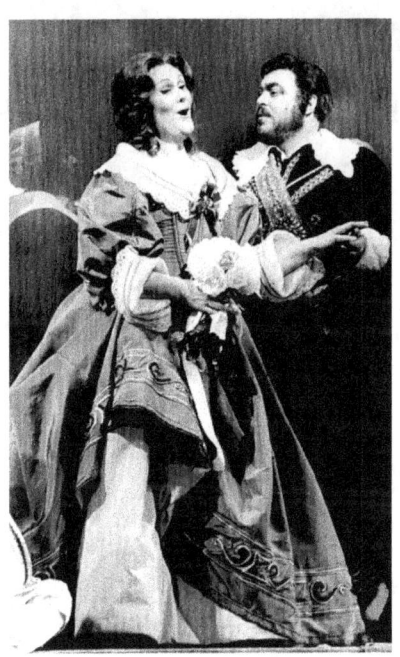
Joan Sutherland and Luciano
Pavarotti in *I Puritani*

beautifully blended together meant so much to me because I had parted from my twin sister when I immigrated to Canada, and perhaps, on hearing those wonderful female voices, there was a longing for the times we spent together in our childhood and young adulthood. What a strange idea.

(The night after I wrote this, I had an odd dream. I was walking down a corridor, and there were people walking toward me and along with me. Ahead of me was a large man. A tall and interesting-looking woman approached, and he stopped her. In the dream, I heard him say, "That line you sing with Analgesia in *Norma* is rubbish. Why don't you just sing la, la, la?" It was quite unlike my usual food and exam-anxiety dreams, enough for me to pause and give it some thought. I actually got on Google and found that the opening words to that amazing duet are "Hear, oh Norma." My birth name was Norma, so what was it I wasn't listening to? What should I have been telling myself? Ah well, that is the way when one questions one's dreams. One is usually left with a few more unanswered questions.)

Marilyn Horne, in a tribute to Sutherland, once said, "We never had to work hard to blend; we both just knew how to listen. And we both wanted the sum of the parts, not the parts. Her voice, with its gorgeous, silver sound, went straight into the ear, with great resonance. People forget how big her voice was." The day after the dream was one of my husband's and my more creative days, and I can only assume the dream was about our relationship when it is at its best. Yes, we both

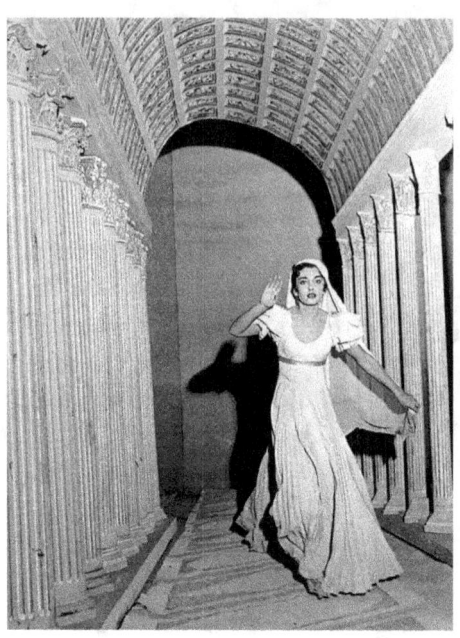

Maria Callas as Giulia in *La Vestale* by Gaspare Spontini

wanted the sum of the parts that day.

Other bel canto singers with the quality of Joan Sutherland are Renato Bruson, José Carreras, Chris Merritt, and Giacomo Aragall, as well as the deceased Alfredo Kraus, Luciano Pavarotti, and Montserrat Caballé.

Opera does seem a curious art form when looked at as a child might, doesn't it? Robertson Davies used the term "childlike" when he wrote of opera. "There is a childlike, unsophisticated quality about opera which commands respect in this wicked world. All that hooting and hollering because somebody has pinched somebody else's girl, or killed the wrong man, or sold his soul to the devil! These are commonplaces in daily life (particularly the latter) and it is astonishing to hear them treated with so much noisy consideration." Clown around as he was wont to do, Davies listened to those Metropolitan Opera broadcasts every Saturday for years, as did I.

One doesn't usually think of Tolstoy as being witty, and maybe he is unintentionally so in his wonderful description of an opera rehearsal, ridiculing (as only Victor Borge has done as well since) the outrageousness of plot, singers, costumes, scenery . . . the whole shebang. Here is his comment on Wagner's *Ring Cycle*: "Sit in the dark for four days in company with people who are not quite normal, and through the auditory nerves subject your brain to the strongest action of the sounds best adapted to excite it, and you'll no doubt be reduced to an abnormal condition and be enchanted by absurdities. But to attain this end you do not even need four days; five hours . . . are quite enough."

Tolstoy was, unlike Robertson Davies, not a big fan of opera because of its eliteness and unavailability to the working man. And while today, opera is readily available to anyone who wants to hear it, the mark of exclusiveness still clings to it.

Lest you think the revived popularity of bel canto died out by the end of the twentieth century, musician and writer Stephen Raskauskas tells us firmly that "Since Rossini sighed that bel canto was lost long ago, he would be pleased that his music has been reclaimed with such fervor in the twenty-first century." (Raskauskas was speaking of a series of bel canto concerts at Carnegie Hall.) "The art of beautiful singing itself, it seems, has been revived alongside bel canto repertoire. And, with divas of the digital age—Ms. DiDonato listed among them—connecting with new audiences around the globe through live broadcasts, this glorious repertoire will thrive for generations to come."

Joyce DiDonato herself waxes eloquent about the art of bel canto singing. "One of the thrills of singing bel canto, as well as one of its great challenges, is rising to the overwhelming vocal demands of this music." She continues, "Its very label bel canto requires a level of beauty that is not always of this world. Part of the joy of this period of music is witnessing the voice do extraordinary things. As singers, the genre requires that we have vocal command over everything—dynamics from feather pianos to radiant fortes, a vocal range that plunges the depths and leaps to the heavens—all the while tossing in expressive trills, rapid coloratura, and melting legato so that the emotional journey of the character comes to vivid life. It's truly the most challenging music for me to sing, and I love it for that reason."

Listening to bel canto reminds me of the amazing facility of the human voice when it comes to expressing our deepest feelings.

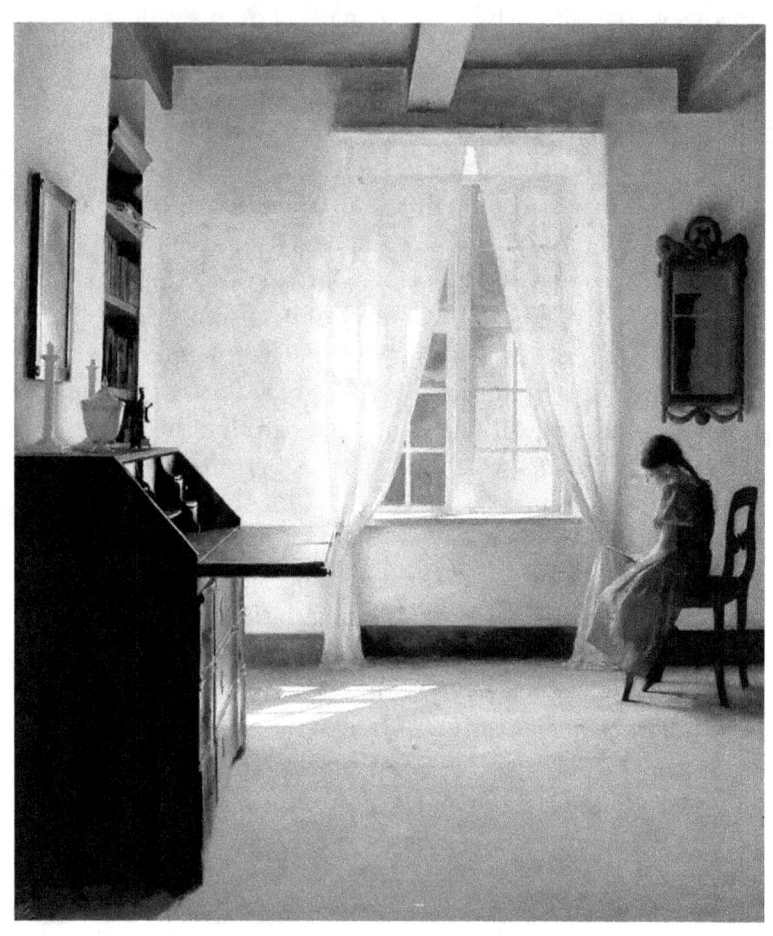

Peter Ilsted, *Interior with Girl Reading*, 1910

the art of
solitude

MY HUSBAND SINGS TO ME IN BED THE SONGS OF HIS
adolescence, downloaded on his MP3 player. I am struck by
the frequency of the word "lonely" in their titles—"Mr. Lonely,"
"Lonely Boy," "Only the Lonely," "Lonely Street," "Never Knew
Lonely," "Lonely Teardrops," "Sgt. Pepper's Lonely Hearts Club
Band." I would have thought it is the present time, with folks
adhered to Facebook and Twitter, their opposing thumbs
brought into full play on iPhones and iPads, for which the
word "loneliness" would be most applicable. I am innocent
of these new methods and outlets for communication, and I
often wonder in amazement what people find to tell each other
all day long. Isn't all that frantic Tweeting and Facebooking
sandbagging their own loneliness? Isn't the present day the
time of the alienated?

When I think of "lonely" in the traditional arts, I think
immediately of Edward Hopper.

Although Hopper complained that "The loneliness thing
is overdone," to me he always seems to be the outsider, the
observer observing the marginal, thus doubling the feeling
of loneliness when we look at his canvases. It's the seeming
inability of people to communicate that, for me, is the
essence of his paintings. Take his painting *Sun in an Empty
Room*, which seems to reflect a deep separateness. About
that painting Hopper commented, "I'm after me." Surely
that is the statement of loneliness. C. S. Lewis said, "We
are born helpless. As soon as we are fully conscious, we

discover loneliness. We need others physically, emotionally, intellectually; we need them if we are to know anything, even ourselves." Perhaps this is what Hopper was trying to express.

John Updike felt Hopper was always on the verge of telling a story. But what was that story? For some, Hopper was the painter of light, but for others he perfectly reflected David Riesman's book, *The Lonely Crowd*, which analyzed the loneliness of humanity within the urban daily rush.

Lonely times are familiar to us all. They only become a problem when we get stuck in loneliness and all the negativity surrounding it. Lonely people have tried—or maybe not tried—to integrate, but can't blend into the world, can't even make real contact. In reality, they may actually be excluded from society for various reasons, but that exclusion can only add to the feeling that lonely people have of being unimportant, having nobody who cares about them, and feeling that in some way they are unworthy. Such a state can lead to despair.

Solitude isn't loneliness; it's different. With solitude, you belong to yourself. With loneliness, you belong to no one. You choose solitude, you drift into loneliness. When you experience loneliness, you're not happy about being alone; the reverse is true when you experience solitude. Solitude is a paradox, for in its depths one realizes that, though alone, one is linked to everything.

Loneliness is being painfully alone, existing in an impoverished state, and feeling that the action is always somewhere over there. I remember after a long meditation period abroad, on the liner coming home, friends knocked on my cabin door and asked me why I wasn't where the action was. I recall telling them, "The action is here." On looking back, I see that moment as a very liberating one.

Isolation kills. It can certainly tip one into illness. The obvious one is depression, and anxiety follows on its heels. Solitude is the enriched state of being alone. But it is not just being on your own. Solitude is you experiencing yourself, providing yourself with sufficient company. You can attain the state of solitude by having a certain independence from day-to-day matters. We need solitude to find a balance that daily life knocks askew.

As a creative person, one needs solitude because one can't be creative if on tap twenty-four hours a day. An original mind needs solitude. Solitude is ground zero for a writer. It's where our Muse hangs out; in solitude, she sends me fresh insights and stimulates my imagination, gives me leads on new ideas for poems and essays. Times of solitude replenish. I don't crave or even think about being elsewhere or with other people. By experiencing the richness of solitude, we can return to the world feeling generous enough to reach out to others.

Once I belonged to a choir, and one evening at practice I suddenly had a small epiphany. It was that when I was able to hear myself, the choir disappeared into the background. I would feel fine for a while, then wobble a little and feel a need to tune my ears to the choir. That was good until, in time, I lost my own voice. Life is a teeter-totter like that. Aloneness, community, aloneness, community.

Our doors are locked, our yards are fenced; even in apartment blocks we often don't know our neighbors. We get in our cars and go wherever we have to go, shutting out everything we pass on the way. In a 2004 survey quoted by John T. Cacioppo and William Patrick in *Loneliness and the Human Need for Social Connection*, twenty-five percent of people answered the question "How many confidants do you have?" with the answer "None."

We have friends who live in a city apartment. Every time we visit, I linger in the lobby where Hopper's painting of an usherette in a cinema is suitably hung alone on one wall. The light is interesting, that is true, but it is the portrayal of people seeking to overcome loneliness by getting lost in movies that interests me. Even the usherette is isolated as audience members lose their lives into that of those portrayed on the screen.

How to reconnect? Loneliness isn't easy to push out of the way. You can't just tell someone to get some friends. You have to feel your loneliness and feel it intensely. Then small steps can be taken.

Sitting in a park instead of in front of the TV; holding your head up and smiling at people you feel good about; helping someone with their shopping bags or to cross heavily trafficked roads—this is the beginning of the road out.

But the art of solitude is not about dealing with extreme loneliness. It is about making your time alone meaningful and creative, so that when you are back in a social milieu, everyone benefits from your refreshed being. The art of solitude can be learned, just as one can learn watercolor painting or flower arranging. Solitude is an important art since it is a win-win activity. You profit creatively by your times of solitude, and the people you meet with when you come back into social situations benefit because by learning to go more deeply into yourself, you are also learning how to listen to others more intently and to respond to them with a greater sensitivity.

My husband and I once lived in an apartment in the middle of a big city. We rarely saw our neighbors and had no friends in the building. Our lives revolved around our work. Gradually this situation caused unease, one that we were smart enough to recognize. We realized that we were being drained by the city and work demands. We felt isolated from our authentic selves. We needed to find solitude. We didn't express it this way, of course. These words came years later, on reflection. Olivier Laing in "Me, myself and I," published in 2012 in *Aeon,* tells of this isolation so well, "Something funny happens to people who are lonely. The lonelier they get, the less adept they become at navigating social currents. Loneliness grows around them, like mold or fur, a prophylactic that inhibits contact, no matter how badly contact is desired. Loneliness is accretive, extending and perpetuating itself. Once it becomes impacted, it isn't easy to dislodge."

How did we find more time for solitude? We moved to the country. Owning land and having a garden meant I had to observe nature a little more carefully than I had done in the past. I gradually became aware of the rhythm of the seasons and of the coming into being and passing away of harvests. Those ritual patterns are the first steps to profiting from time alone. I didn't alienate my husband by seeking my own time, because I explained to him what I needed to do. I write for a living and have committed myself to doing this full-time. I need solitude to work out writing solutions and approach my topics in fresh ways.

Nowadays, I only answer emails once a day, in the early morning, and I switch the machine off at 5 p.m. I don't have a TV and never got hooked on computer games or the social networks that substitute superficial meetings with in-depth encounters. I take my household chores seriously, having learned that time alone scrubbing the kitchen floor is as good for creativity as wandering in a bee-loud glade. I have learned to stay with silence, no background music pretending to calm me. In effect, I have redesigned my life. At the same time as I learned to find and use solitude, I entered my island community life; the first time I had ever lived in community. Maybe the positive solitude helped me to be brave enough to connect at some depth, as I had never done before.

Mastering the art of solitude is a way of controlling and transmuting loneliness, giving your isolation meaning so that it allows you to also give more meaning to your relationships in the community. When I think of solitude these days, I immediately think of the little island I have settled on and a nearby beach at sunset after the tourists have left.

With the world seeming to spin faster and faster, powered, it seems, by our pointless communications that aren't able to bring us any nearer to each other, we feel irritated and unsatisfied. Even in a crowd we feel unfulfilled and lonely. Times of solitude can bring us back to a certain balance.

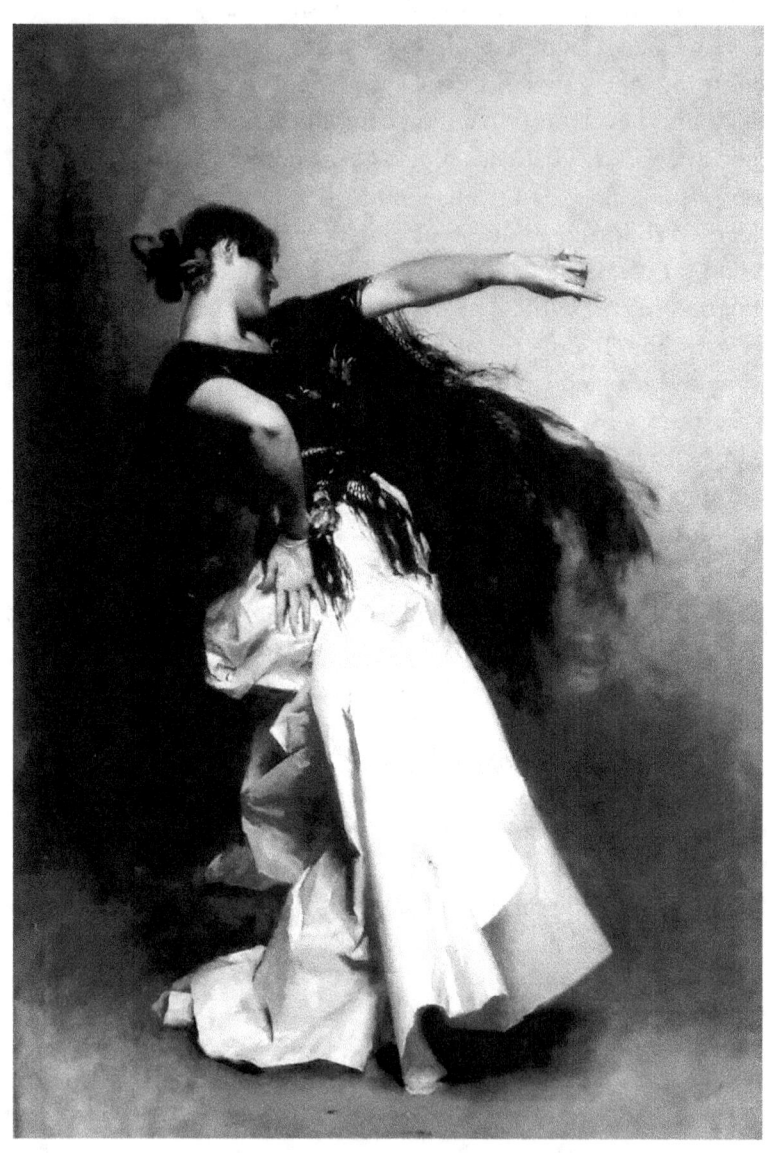

John Singer Sargent, *Spanish Dancer*, 1880

the art of
flamenco

WHEN I WAS A CHILD, MY FATHER OFTEN TOOK MY TWIN
and me through apple orchards down to the fields where the
Gypsies were encamped. I had no idea what drew him down
there or why I remember those walks so fondly. As an adult, I
never romanticized the Gypsy life. I know what it is to be an
outsider. Homelessness, having to always be moving on I was
to experience only much later in life. Still, the vagabond life of
an outsider was somewhere in my blood. I wrote a poem about
those early walks, which I dedicated to my father (p. 118).

My imagined freedom of the Gypsies disappeared
underground as I went to university, got my degree, married,
and had children. Occasionally, I would catch glimpses of it,
such as when I first attended a performance by the Moiseyev
dancers to find that their much theatricized Russian folk
dances stirred something inside me.

My first wedding consisted of a small group of friends
eating hors d'oeuvre after a registry office marriage. For
my second wedding, a large gathering of folks in wild and
exotic folk costume were led through exotic folk dances that
had them spinning. I danced for the guests wearing a silk,
maroon-colored dress (perhaps from Morocco) with heavy
gold edging. A Russian peasant scarf over my head was topped
with a silk cloth to match the dress, and the scarf and cloth
were held in place with a belly-dance headpiece of ornamental
metal. My necklace I made myself, having drilled holes into
many one-cent coins (through the Queen's face I hesitate to

Gypsies

I was seven or maybe eight
when I went with my father
to see the drifting Gypsies.
My memories are a jumble
of clothespins, tinkered
kettles and stolen apples
and a strange excitement
that I didn't yet recognize.
Yet something still lingers of
that day; clear as a Fall morning
snatched from right and wrong;
and that's the feel of my small
hand in his as we walked together
each seeking in our own way
an imagined freedom,
through the laden orchards
to their campsite.

admit) and strung them together with maroon silk ribbon.

The previous couple of years I had earnestly studied flamenco. At first, I was a student of a dancer whose claim to fame was that she had been a flamenco dancer in some shipboard cabaret in a movie whose title I have forgotten. My second teacher was almost totally, ferociously authentic since she had studied in Spain and our classes were accompanied by her flamenco-guitar-playing husband. I say "almost" since she was Canadian, which certainly tempered her temperament in this, our most reasonable of countries. She didn't lack passion, however. Once, in a rage, she threw a bun she was eating at her husband, our guitar-playing accompanist. Now that's *duende!*

My grandfather's cousin had a Gypsy orchestra that accompanied his wife singing mournful songs and his daughters doing wild dances. As a child, I longed to dance with them and wear those red boots and embroidered costumes. As for my progress as a flamenco dancer, I never did master the castanets, and within a few years I had exhausted my mid-life-crisis dance career in favor of building an earth-sheltered house. Although I have no idea where my collection of flamenco records went, or my polka-dotted, frilled dress for that matter, the rough voice of the flamenco singer stayed

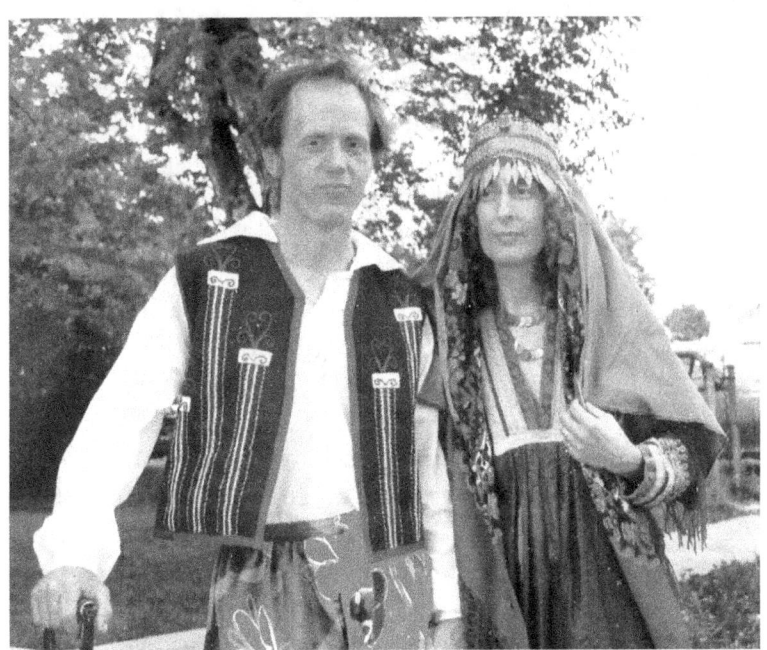

Naomi and Elias in dancing garb on their wedding day

with me, and the flamenco rhythms stayed somewhere around
my now gum-boot-shod feet.

Dance may well have pre-dated speech as a form of
communication. I like to think it was that way for the body
is a fine instrument to use to express joy, anger, ecstasy, or
fear. In flamenco, however, it was the song that appeared
first, accompanied by handclapping, rapping of knuckles on
the table, and finger snapping. The dance, performed by the
bailaor, and the guitar, played by the *tocaor*, were added later.

It is believed that flamenco came with the Gypsy tribes
who, after their expulsion from India around the ninth
century, eventually settled in Andalusia, a portion of southern
Spain, by the 1400s. But even there, their persecution
continued and they took to the mountains. It was in those
heights that their vocabulary of songs and dances developed
as they told of their misery, rejection, betrayal, hatred , and
despair.

If ever raw emotion found form, it is in flamenco song,
sung by the *cantaor*. Flamenco song was an early form of the

blues in extremis. "Anguish made flesh," as Garcia Lorca put it. The flamenco song expressed a fear of death, a desire for love, and a rage to live, despite their sorrows. I should note that not all flamenco song and dance is of this *cante grande* style. There are also more lighthearted and even joyful songs and dances.

The Gypsies were joined by other outsiders, such as the Spanish *conversos*—Jews who had to convert to Christianity—and *moriscos*—Moors similarly marginalized. Within the Gypsy group, they practiced their religions in secret and learned to express their suffering in song and dance. In the late eighteenth century, these persecuted people came out of hiding, and their strange songs and dances, a mixture of elements of Gypsy, Moorish, Jewish, and Indian culture, found a ready audience in the Iberian peninsula. The accentuation of hand and arm movements in flamenco so clearly links it to traditional Indian dance forms. The Moors, too, emphasized the upper body in their dance, for Islam forbade drawing attention to the feet. It was much later that the fast footwork of flamenco came to the fore. It is said that the flamenco heel tapping fastens the dancer to death, the arm movements, to love.

As flamenco left the Gypsy communities and came out into the open, the *cafés cantantes* came into being; these were cafés where flamenco was an added attraction to the food and beverages served. The peak of their popularity was between 1860 and 1915. It was in these cafés that flamenco dance came to the fore. By the last half of the nineteenth century, these cafés were flourishing in Seville, Granada, Barcelona, and Madrid. As flamenco moved, so it started to incorporate local folk songs wherever it went, for example, in the *malagueñas*. These hybrid songs were preferred by non-Gypsy singers, but the true Gypsies stayed with the *cante grande* and its raw passion.

Flamenco artists started to be viewed as professionals and some gained fame and all its accoutrements. Later, flamenco became a theatrical performance and, in such a situation, the original anguish and pain were hard to maintain. Improvisation disappeared as steps became more precise. Grammatical Spanish came to replace the Gypsy expressions, and people began, as flamenco softened, to find its original harshness displeasing. Flamenco became a socially acceptable art form, and when this happens, in whatever art form, its power is destroyed. However, dancers like Carmen Amayo reinvigorated the form. It is she who usurped the male dancer's footwork, excelling in it herself and even wearing male costume. In early flamenco, as I mentioned, it was the hand and arm movements that were accentuated in female dancers. In the film *Gypsy Heart*, there is a marvelous moment when Amayo is shown rapping out the rhythms of the dance with her knuckles on an old wooden table. Even her hands spoke passionately.

In the 1950s, professional flamenco companies started to tour outside Spain, and paradoxically, *aficionados* started to search for performers closer to flamenco's origins. So, in a circuitous way, the theatricization of flamenco brought a resurgence of the true form.

Castanets, which, as I mentioned, I never mastered, were a later addition, and many felt them unnecessary for they distracted from the arm and hand movements. In my own practice, I did better with the *palmas* (clapping) and the finger snapping that encourages the dancer.

In flamenco, the dancer, singer, and guitarist are all closely linked as they energize each other. During moments when the singers and dancers are not performing, they embolden the others with *Olés* and the rhythmic clapping of hands and finger snapping. The singer, the dancer, and the guitarist cue and react to each other's improvisations. Is it my strange mind that links the anguished *Ay!* that starts so many flamenco songs (the *quejío*) with the sorrowful *Oy!* that prefaces so many Jewish laments?

Alegrías, Bulerías, Bulerías por Soleá, Cartageneras, Fandango, Fandango de Huelva, Fandango Malageño, Granaínas, Malagueñas, Mineras, Rondeñas, Rumba, Saeta, Seguiriyas, Sevillanas, Soleá por Bulerías, Tangos, Tanguillos, Tientos, Villancicos . . . the names of the flamenco dances are entrancing, although I mastered none of them; and, in fact, our beginners' class, with the fiery bun-throwing teacher, was so bad that we weren't even allowed to perform in the end-of-term concert. I didn't care because I had learned what I wanted from the lessons: permission to express my feelings with my body. The proud stance of the dancer set my shoulders back, immeasurably improving my posture, as I arched in a certain pride. After forty years of placating others, it was so liberating to let my self express what it wanted to say. The strange enchantment of non-Western music, with its smaller-than-semitone intervals, and the wearing of exotic costume worked small miracles on the inhibited middle-class housewife of those years that I was. The discipline of endless hours practicing prepared me, in a way, for the discipline of the endless hours of writing I was to do later in life.

Flamenco is not really a dance for the young. It is perfect for the maturing person and many dancers continue into their seventies. Yes, flamenco is the dance for the prime of life, when the joys and pains of living have made some mark on the performer. It is the perfect dance form to see one over one's middle years. Sagging breasts, loose stomach muscles, varicose-veined legs, none of these things matter when one is lost in telling the world of all one has been through in the discipline of stamping one's feet and moving one's arms and tossing one's head.

What was it that drew me—a rather inhibited, just-separated-from-my-first-husband, and still rather house-wifey being—to such a passionate dance form? Well, I suppose it was the search for a passion lacking in my own life. At that time, I can remember feeling that I was moving through a life that was not under my control, that my feet were merely skimming the ground, and that my whole being was living some kind of strange reality that I hadn't chosen. My flamenco studies were my sub-conscious desire to be part of something rough and real and fully expressing the feelings that were hidden inside me. In my outside life, as I gained confidence in what small skills I had to offer the world, flamenco gave me added strength.

Still, even after my flamenco studies, I lacked *duende*,

the quality Garcia Lorca described as "a power which climbs up inside the performer from the soles of the feet, the spirit of the earth which scorches the artists and produces an inspired performance." I'm afraid Lorca was accused of romanticizing the flamenco performer and that the intensity he saw and heard was more likely caused by alcohol and drug consumption during the *juerga* (the group gathering when flamenco is performed). Well . . . maybe. Still, I sense that quality of *duende*, of intensity, is still somewhat missing in my writing and in my life as I sit pertly on life's edge, surveying all with a somewhat cynical eye.

Only once in my whole life has the rough, desperate sound of *cante grande* ever come from my own throat. It was when a person close to me was dangerously ill. When I heard the news, the sound came spontaneously out, a wild, raw sound, an animal cry.

And knowing there is something lacking in my understanding of flamenco I write:

flamenco isn't danced by
learning flamenco, flamenco is danced
by living flamenco
flamenco isn't Sophia Loren
flamenco is Anna Magnani

I have been a skimmer through life, detached from my body at birth, *ego sum umbra*, a will-o-the-wisp. The solid grounding I found in the flamenco form for a few years reminded me that the ground is under my feet, and it is this ground that I must walk on this time around.

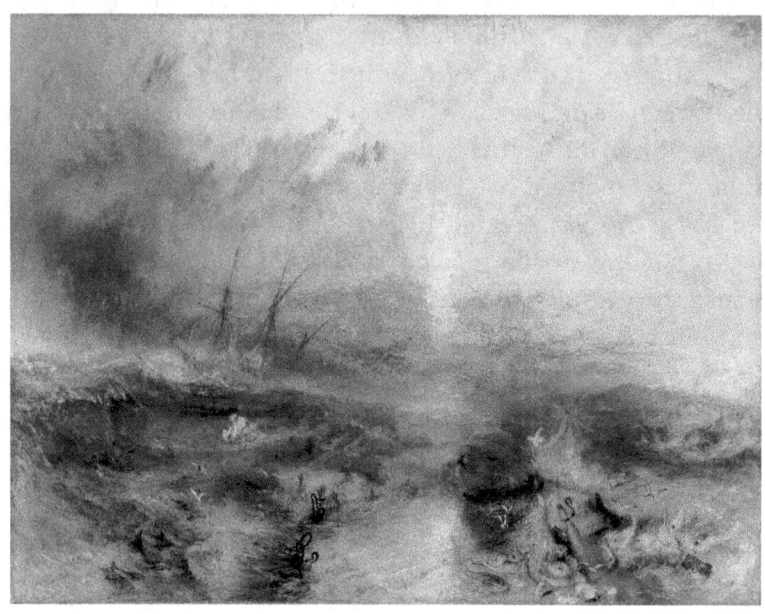

J. M. W. Turner, *Slavers Throwing Overboard the Dead and Dying*, 1840

It is a sunset on the Atlantic after prolonged storm; but the storm is partially lulled, and the torn and streaming rain clouds are moving in scarlet lines to lose themselves in the hollow of the night. The whole surface of the sea included in the picture is divided into two ridges of enormous swell, not high, nor local, but a low, broad heaving of the whole ocean, like the lifting of its bosom by deep-drawn breath after the torture of the storm. Between these two ridges, the fire of the sunset falls along the trough of the sea, dyeing it with an awful but glorious light, the intense and lurid splendor which burns like gold and bathes like blood.

—John Ruskin

the art of
ekphrasis

EKPHRASIS ORIGINALLY MEANT THE DESCRIBING OF
objects, even though they might be imaginary, in a way that
the reader could easily picture them. The word comes from
the Greek *ekphrazein*, composed of *ek-* (out) plus *phrazein* (to
recount, to describe, to explain).

Ekphrasis can also apply to any medium being used to
describe and enhance another. When it comes to describing
works of art, ekphrasis can be composed such that the writer
is speaking to the work of art; the work of art is speaking
for itself; the writer is describing the work of art in detail or
speaking of the ideas, emotions, and feelings that the work
gives rise to; or the writer is speaking of the moment when
the work is being viewed—the work in its momentary setting.
Modern ekphrasis often describes the process of making the
work of art as well as actually describing it. Ekphrasis can also
be writing about a piece of music or music composed about
art, such as Jacob Gilboa's composition *Twelve Glass Windows
of Chagall in Jerusalem* for voice and instruments.

In its early usage, ekphrasis was used more for describing
objects than art works. As W. J. T. Mitchell, a professor of art
history, points out, "Goblets, urns, vases, chests, cloaks, girdles,
various sorts of weapons and armor, and architectural ornaments
like friezes, reliefs, frescoes and statues *in situ* provide the first
objects of ekphrastic description probably because the detachment
of painting as an isolated, autonomous, and movable object of
aesthetic contemplation is a relatively late development in the

visual arts." While used in the Classics—Homer's description of Achilles's shield in *The Iliad* is often given as an example—examples of ekphrasis are frequent in the nineteenth century when the general public rarely had a chance to travel to see ancient ruins or Renaissance paintings. Nineteenth-century writers John Ruskin, William Hazlitt, and Walter Pater were known for vivid descriptions of actual art works, so vivid that the reader could almost feel they were looking at the work in question. Of course, these non-Classical uses of ekphrasis often included the writer's personal reaction to the work of art as well as a striking description. Read a section from Ruskin's description of J. M. W. Turner's *Slavers Throwing Overboard the Dead and Dying* (p. 124).

Nowadays, accurate color-plates can be produced for most works of art, and the Internet allows the whole world to view them easily. The description of the work is thus no longer so necessary. Page 127 shows a painting by Alice Rich titled "Dissolve" and an ekphrastic piece that I wrote and use when giving workshops on ekphrastic writing.

A comparatively recent example of ekphrasis is John Updike's lovely little essay on Antonella da Messina's *St. Jerome in His Study*, which expands one's understanding of the piece by giving it a story. Ekphrasis does tend to invent or elaborate, sometimes didactically, using the painting to point out the right way to live or the right way to die.

As I mentioned earlier, ekphrasis covers the description of not only actual works of art, but imaginary ones, such as Keats's Grecian Urn. Other literary examples of words describing works of art are Oscar Wilde's *The Picture of Dorian Gray* and Dostoevsky's *The Idiot*, in which Prince Myshkin sees a painting of a dead Christ that deeply affects him. Poets frequently use ekphrasis—Yeats in "Leda and the Swan"; Marianne Moore in "Sea Unicorns and Land Unicorns"; Adrienne Rich in "Mourning Picture"; W. D. Snodgrass in "Matisse: *The Red Studio*"; Rosanna Warren in "Renoir" (about that painter's *Luncheon of the Boating Party*); Donald Hall in "Listen" (about Edward Munch's *The Scream*); Anne Sexton in "The Starry Night" (about Van Gogh's painting of the same name); and Richard Wilbur, who did a witty take on Pieter de Hooch's *Dutch Courtyard*, with a poem using the same name. When it comes to

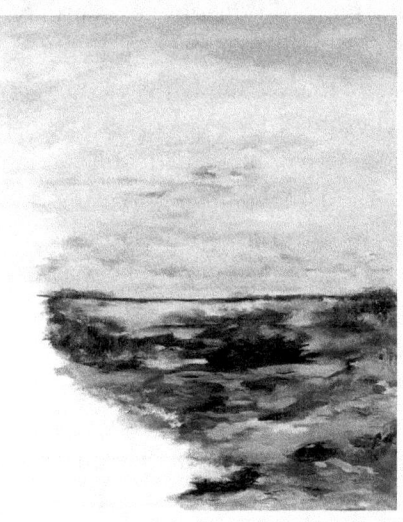

Alice Rich, *Dissolve*

This painting, appropriately called *Dissolve*, is primarily divided into two equal parts, divided by a somewhat uneven dark-line horizon. Both parts are painted very loosely. The sky is neither clear, nor stormy, though a few clouds are drifting across it. The ground also is amorphous. It could be marshland or sandy, and appears to have clumps of grass distributed irregularly over it. This mysterious landscape is further puzzling because the left-hand lower corner is blank canvas. At first the ground seems to arise slowly from the edges of the naked canvas, but taking the title into consideration, one could also say that the blank canvas is eating into the landscape and thus dissolving it. Either way, this desolate scene captivates with the many questions that arise from viewing it.

—Naomi Beth Wakan

writing on photography, Ted Hughes's poetry about Fay Godwin's *Elmet* or Peter Keen's *River* are good examples.

Elizabeth Bergmann Loizeaux did a nice take on poets and ekphrasis when she said that ekphrasis helps us recognize "how a work of art that promises refuge from the world ends up sending the poet back out into it." Many examples can be read in John Hollander's brilliant book on ekphrastic poetry, *The Gazer's Spirit*. It would seem almost every twentieth-century poet has done at least one poem in ekphrastic style.

Photography, film, TV, and digital processing have made us a "seeing" culture, and maybe this shift from words to images has been subconsciously felt as a threat to writers, particularly poets. So they have, as it were, embraced the enemy in order to survive. However, although a competitive element might subtly be there, ekphrasis is more like a friendship. Ekphrasis isn't just a description; it's a relationship.

Ekphrastic writing introduces ideas of movement and sound that weren't able to be shown in the actual painting. Writing is eloquent and active, whereas art is concerned with space, silence, and stillness. Murray Krieger said, "Ekphrasis craves the spatial fix." In ekphrasis, the writing shouldn't just decorate the work of art, however, but deepen it and equal it in intensity.

All that being said, W. J. T. Mitchell nicely points out the impossibility of ekphrasis's aims, for "A verbal representation cannot represent, that is, make present its object in the same way a visual representation can. It may refer to an object, describe it, invoke it, but it can never bring its visual presence before us in the way pictures do. Words can 'cite,' but never 'sight' their objects." He then modifies this situation by saying, "the impossibility of ekphrasis is overcome in imagination or metaphor, when we discover a 'sense' in which language can do what so many writers have wanted it to do: 'make us see.'" Referring to the words of William Carlos Williams from a poem entitled "Song," Mitchell quotes and comments, "'The ear and the eye lie/down together in the same bed,' lulled by 'undying accents.' The estrangement of the image/text division is overcome, and a sutured, synthetic form, a verbal icon or imagetext, arises in its place."

Of course, painting has a "nowness" that words cannot have. It is a more immediate and a more direct description of the artist's outer (or inner) reality. Ekphrastic writing intercedes between the work of art and the viewer and so can either impede or deepen the message. It is as if the writing is giving voice to a silent art. I love James Merrill's advice on ekphrasis, "The poet who would write on a work of art must listen for its opening words."

Author Mai Al-Nakib accentuates the "exchange" nature of ekphrasis. "Ekphrasis," she explains, "exposes the mutability of forms, since, by definition, it is the expression of one form in terms of another. Any form that is expressed in terms of another always sweeps elements of its former composition along with it even as it is itself substantially transformed. In this sense,

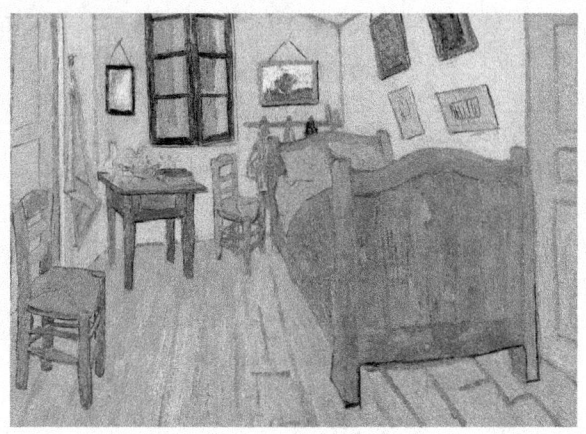

Vincent van Gogh, *Bedroom in Arles*, 1888

My bedside books are dreams to drink,
paths to lap up, absinthe to imbibe.
I have reading glasses now,
and tall stacks of books seem as rickety as me,
till a new bookcase finds room in the house.
The carpet is more worn from the door to the bed
than ever before, nights of reading
distorting the pillow trapped under my side.
The tiny lamp I use keeps my wife
from waking, and somehow words
show me the road where I will go.

In Arles, the painter's room has no dreams,
no carpet or books, or glasses to speak of
old age. The bed just wide enough
for a single man, its only dreams
may be the colours in paintings
hung carelessly on vivid walls,
yet the window stays closed
to tomorrow.

Even a bullet to the chest
cannot end
such bookless, dreamless sadness.

—Michael Dylan Welch

ekphrasis always involves an 'exchange.'" The work of art already describes a reality, and so, when the writer writes about the work of art, it is almost as if he/she is entering a dialogue with the artist about a reality twice removed from them. Professor Elizabeth Bergmann Loizeaux suggests that painting is a kind of portal into the past or other spaces when she states, "The history that modern ekphrasis opens up is a history made by the artist and remade by the viewer/poet." Lawrence Felinghetti did a nice description of the intertwining of the arts in ekphrasis when he wrote, "Monet never knew / he was painting his "Lilies" for / a lady from the Chicago Art Institute / who went to France and filmed / today's lilies / by the "bridge of Giverny"/ a leaf afloat among them."

It is also possible to reverse the usual direction (where the art work inspires the writing) of ekphrasis. Charles Demuth's painting *The Figure 5 in Gold* was inspired by William Carlos Williams's poem "The Great Figure."

Also, as has been said, it's not just written text that constitutes ekphrasis. In her book *Musical Ekphrasis*, Siglind Bruhn writes of the exploration that recent composers have taken in the use of music for the enrichment of visual representation. She also gives examples of musical ekphrasis with dance and with text. Bruhn says that while "program music" could be an overall title for it— with its storms, onomatopoeic attempts, and pastoral scenes— program music merely illustrates externals whereas real musical ekphrasis would reveal the deeper levels. "Program music presents, musical ekphrasis re-presents" another art form. Bruhn points out that Mussorgsky's *Pictures at an Exhibition* is really a hybrid, not digging deeply into each painting, but presenting a whole picture of an exhibition, including the promenading steps of the viewer. Bruhn insists that in ekphrasis the two elements must be able to stand alone. For example:

- *Parade* by Jean Cocteau, Erik Satie, Léonide Massine, and Pablo Picasso was a cooperative effort and not ekphrasis.

- William Blake's art and poetry, Arnold Schoenberg's music and poetry, and Kurt Schwitters's music and poetry are examples of ekphrasis, according to Bruhn.

- Paul Klee's *Twittering Machine* was used by several musicians—Gunther Schuller, Jasha Klebe, and Maxwell Davies.

- *The Rake's Progress* was a double ekphrasis, as W. H. Auden and Daniel Kallman did the libretto from a series of William Hogarth etchings, and Igor Stravinsky was inspired to give them a musical interpretation.

- Another double ekphrasis was Jean-Antoine Watteau's *fêtes galantes* (a type of painting, small in scale, featuring elegantly attired men and women engaged in amorous play often in park-like settings), which inspired Paul Verlaine to write an ekphrastic poem; and from this, Claude Debussy wrote an ekphrastic piece of music, *Clair de lune*.

- Marc Chagall's stained glass windows in the Hadassah-Hebrew University Medical Center gave rise to several musical ekphrases, including John McCabe's *The Chagall Windows*; Petr Eben's *Okna*; and, as mentioned earlier, Jacob Gilboa's *Twelve Glass Windows of Chagall in Jerusalem*.

Ekphrasis in whatever form adds layers of insight to the work it is describing, whether it is writing about art, music describing poetry, or dance adding meaning to music. These days, with gallery tours filled with commentaries and written accompaniment to the paintings and sculpture, ekphrasis becomes the oral added to the writing added to the silent painting. In fact, many recent works of art have music, words, and dance intermingling with the painting or sculpture, so ekphrasis fades into multimedia presentations, and it becomes difficult to sort out what is enriching what. But as long as enrichment is taking place, let's just wait and see what form ekphrasis might take next.

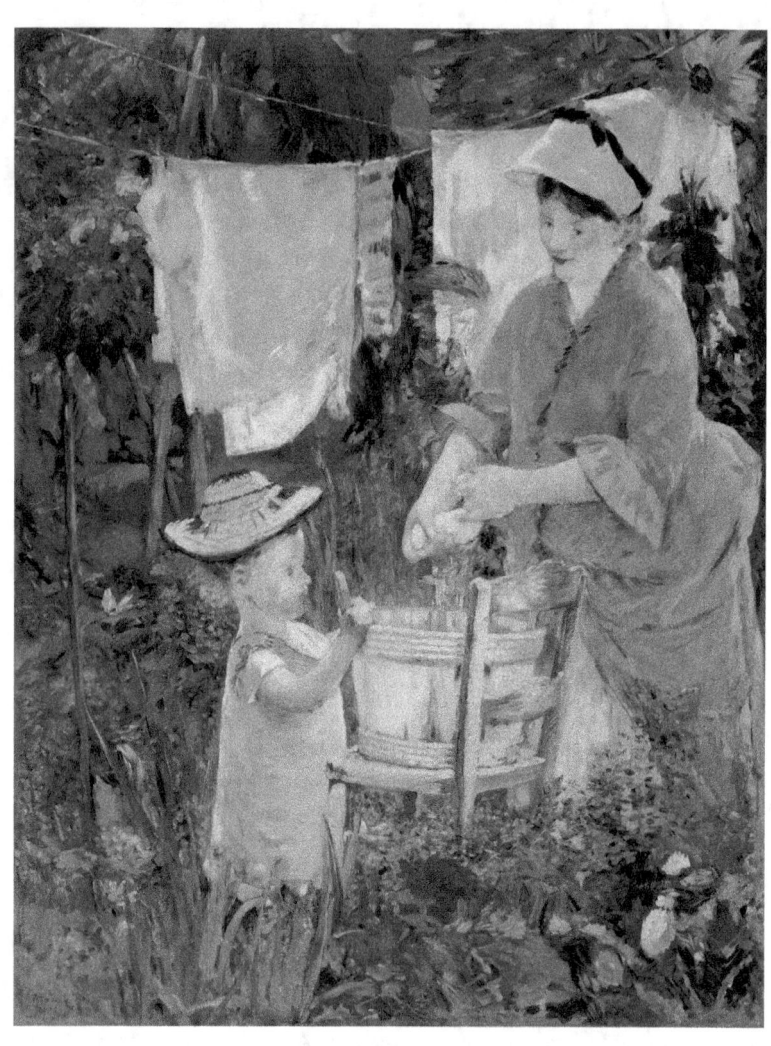

Édouard Manet, *Laundry*, 1875

the art of
domesticity

I WONDER WHETHER IT ISN'T HUMAN NATURE TO rationalize, to justify our moves in life after we have taken them, to somehow make our choices seem reasonable, even virtuous. I am pondering this idea as I have recently decided to choose the art of domesticity as my next exploration in life. At eighty-eight, I no longer fly or drive and am even reluctant to leave our little island of Gabriola to ferry to Vancouver Island. To take a further one-and-a-half-hour ferry ride to Vancouver—at any time in the near future—seems very unlikely. I ignore stories of folks my age taking their first parachute jump or paddling the Grand Canyon. Unlike them, my horizons have definitely moved into our backyard—a small orchard of fruit trees and berry patches and a rather reluctant vegetable garden. That, and our household duties, my husband and I can just about manage.

So my next focus will be on the domestic front rather than the world stage, and my late-life career will be to practice the art of domesticity. Not that I haven't tried my hand at it before. In the 1950s I exemplified the obedient wife; a *Joy of Cooking* and Betty Crocker kind of person with a frilly apron tied firmly about my waist. I straddled between the world where the man was the wage-earner and the female offered domestic support, and that other world, the world of women breaking through the glass ceiling. I fit into neither world completely. Sixty years since my first attempt at the art of domesticity, the world is definitely different. Anyone of any gender can be an accepted and valued practitioner, and while a familiarity with the basic skills of cooking, cleaning, doing laundry, and gardening still remain—not to mention a passing knowledge of electrical, plumbing, and small engine repairs—the art of domesticity these days blends in with recent moves towards *lagom* (Swedish word meaning "just the right amount" or "in moderation"), wabi-sabi / feng-shui interior design, *hygge* (Danish and Norwegian word meaning "coziness and contentment"), and the living of an ethical lifestyle.

Could it be that for a rare moment I am in sync with the rest of the world? It feels strange, but somehow satisfactory.

The art of domesticity as I see it, makes the home not just a place for rest and respite from a demanding and often confusing world, but involves creating a space, a comfortable space, where creativity finds fertile soil and some kind of sense can be made of our lives. The art of domesticity doesn't just see that basic needs are met, but creates an environment where talents are nurtured and where the folks who share the space interact at a deeper level with their material surroundings—the old wooden cooking spoons, the hand-knitted couch throw, the vase of peeled silver dollars—such things linking us to nature outside and taking us deeper into our own nature within. This art, as other arts, demands a great respect for its tools—the stove, the fridge, spades and rakes, the sewing machine, the ironing board, the darning mushroom.

The art of domesticity is the art of creating an enriched environment for society's smallest unit, the modern family, however you like to define it. It is a responsible art, an ethical art that fulfills the Buddhist recommendation for right living. The art of domesticity is not just about designing a usable and well-run home, it is about living a useful life. Although happiness and a sense of security may be byproducts, the art of domesticity, as other arts, intensifies meaning, taking the home beyond providing mere shelter and sustenance. Its purpose is personal transformation. It is the art of being involved deeply in your own life.

Just as with any other art, you put yourself fully into the art of domesticity and tell of yourself via the environment you have created. Your mark on your home is as distinctive as a

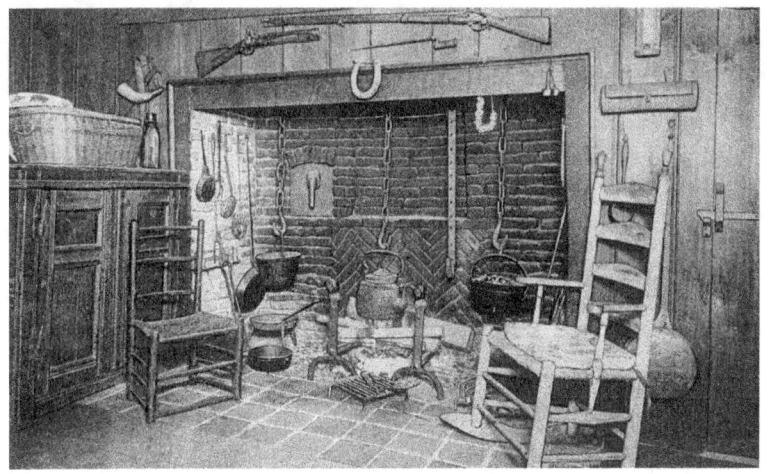

The Kitchen, House of the Seven Gables, Salem, Massachusetts, c. 1940

Dali or a Picasso. It is your style. And just as with any other art, there are times of extreme monotonous duties—bathrooms that continually need cleaning, endless loads of wash to drop into the washing machine, meals that may take hours to prepare only to be eaten in less than one. There will be moments of fatigue and extreme boredom, moments when we feel overwhelmed at the immensity of the art which we have chosen to master—ourselves a Sisyphus on the domestic front. But the painter, the sculptor, the potter, the weaver all have those moments too.

Whether one is a writer, an artist, or a creator of domestic environments, our skills and techniques slowly become part of our muscular system, and this then provides entryways for the bliss of fresh creativity. The real trick to the art of domesticity is not the icing—the floral arrangements, the choice of a painting to go over the couch, things like that—it is how to give value to ritual and repetition. For it's in the small everyday things that success or failure shows—how to make the bed every day as if it had never been made that way before, how to make each meal call out its uniqueness. Simone Weil said, "Attention is the rarest and purest form of generosity." It's our attention to those small everyday things that allows us to add bounteousness to warm our domestic skills.

From the front gate, climbing the stairs or pressing the elevator button, we move from the public space to the private one; changing shoes equals changing moods. Kitchen and dining spaces provide a background for our daily nourishment; the bedroom makes available a place for our necessary rest and intimate contact; and the living room provides a holdall for our family and social life. Each part of the home demands the techniques of the art of domesticity so that spaces not only fulfill their functions, but also restore and re-energize us. Then we can return to the world outside refreshed and optimistic.

The art of domesticity demands the surprises and delights that spontaneity can bring—first spring greens in the pot; first daisies in a kitchen jar; a child's security blanket, no longer needed, but now casually thrown over a chair for all to use. At the same time, the art of domesticity demands foresight and extreme organizational abilities to coordinate even a simple meal and bring it attractively to the table, to see that basic necessities are stocked in the cupboards, that the furniture is comfortable and arranged so as to smooth pathways within and between rooms. Just as music demands organizing notes and writing asks for "the right words in the right order," so the art of domesticity has a large element of organization in it. The beauty of mixed textures, pleasant smells, thoughtful arrangements, relaxing sounds arise when the basics for living have been solidly provided.

As the inside of the home reflects seasonal changes by changes of food, flowers, clothes, food, bedding, we start to move in step with and have a better appreciation of natural cycles outside and the cycles of our own life. We come to appreciate decay and aging as equal to growth and fresh beginnings. We learn to accept the bittersweet conditions of life. We no longer strive for perfection, and we realize that elegance and style can be expressed in simplicity and have nothing to do with the amount of money we have or the glamorousness of our lives. A simple home can feel just as ample and abundant as one with a more flashy display. Those daisies in the kitchen jar can be just as uplifting as orchids in an antique Chinese urn. The greater our skill at domesticity, the less we need to seek power, money, and meaning from the outside world. The art of domesticity can teach us the satisfactoriness of knowing our right size in the universe.

We need the comfort a good home can provide, but we also need that home to provide connections between its inhabitants and with the world outside. We need the home to allow for celebration and for mourning.

Of course the art of domesticity is concerned with things such as adequate lighting and hanging windchimes. Providing aesthetic delight is one of the aims of the art of domesticity, but just as important is the ability to provide an environment that works, an authentic environment.

As in any other art, it is the exploration that counts—the "what if I do it this way, instead of that" kind of curiosity, the combination of different ingredients that have maybe never been combined before.

I'm afraid I won't be a virtuoso in the art of domesticity, not a radical such as Shannon Hayes whose every action on the domestic front seems to have been considered from an ecological and moral point of view. If I were to do that, I would seldom get out of bed in the morning, and even in bed I would worry, as I lay there, that my sheets had maybe been woven in some sweat shop in Bangladesh. However, though some folk may feel the world's woes will be solved politically or by the wide variety of religious beliefs available, I belong to the school who feels they will be tackled one household at a time by we practitioners of the art of domesticity. For individuals who can return home at the end of a hard day not only to a refuge, but also to a place of refreshment, will be sure to return to the outside world the next morning with fresh hope and possibly solutions to the problems that had fretted them the day before.

Considered along with other arts, the art of domesticity might well be described as a long-term happening, a multi-room installation. If you like your art to blend in with your life, as I do, surely pursuing the art of domesticity is a very suitable choice.

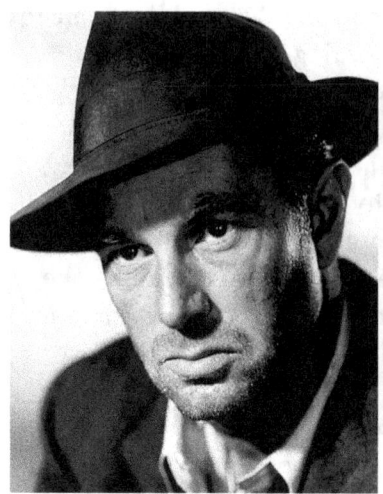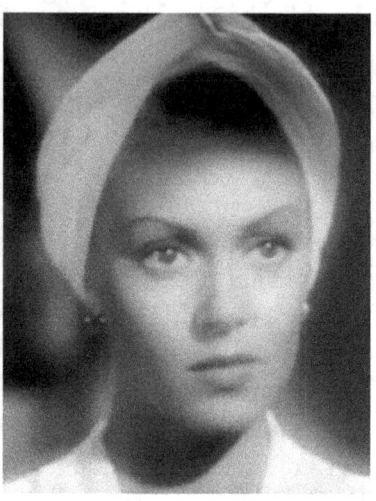

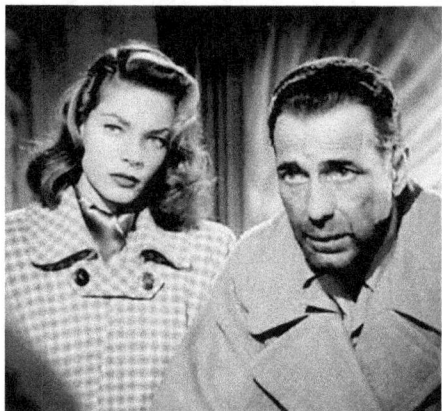

[top left] Studio publicity portrait of Sterling Hayden for the film *The Asphalt Jungle*, 1950 [top right] Screenshot of Lana Turner from the trailer for the film *The Postman Always Rings Twice*, 1946 [bottom] Lauren Bacall and Humphrey Bogart from the film *Dark Passage*, 1947

the art of
film noir

HE THROWS THE DOOR OPEN WIDE. HE IS HANDSOME
beyond words and has the face of a dark angel. She is
startled and rises hesitantly from her chaise lounge. She is
slender, platinum blond, and gorgeous. Sparks should be
flying between them any moment now as they rush into an
embrace in the center of the room. Instead, he reaches into
the pocket of his belted trench coat while she opens her
beaded purse. Two shots ring out at the same time, and they
come together in the center of the floor, joined in a pool of
blood. Such was the way with the film genre you might have
watched in the late forties and the fifties of the last century
and watched again more recently on DVDs; the genre is
known as film noir.

Film noir characters all seemed to be fleeing from
something in the past or something a little more substantial
in the present. What this was would often be revealed later
in the film by way of flashbacks. In film noir, whatever the
protagonists are fleeing from overcomes and defeats them in
the end.

Film noir disobeyed everything that Hollywood
represented—the chronological plot, the happy family in the
adorable house with a white picket fence, the American dream.
Film noir movies were about the underbelly of the American
dream. They were about losers, no matter how beautiful the
bodies involved. The censorship code at that time—the years
stretching from the 1941 *Maltese Falcon* to the 1958 *Touch of*

Evil—demanded that evil not go unpunished, so some films had to have extra scenes added to meet this requirement. That the innocent died with the guilty only made the films extra noir. Another ruling of the Hollywood code at that time was that a person couldn't be shown in bed with anyone but their spouse. Not all films noir were without a wish for redemption, however. One character in *Walk Softly Stranger* says, "I just want a nice house with a front lawn I can mow . . . without getting mowed down myself."

The elements of film noir were the flawed hero (the cop gone wrong, the good man forced into doing evil) and, almost always, the femme fatale, who would never be seen in a kitchen cooking or nestling a baby, but usually had a drink in one hand and a cigarette in the other, dropping either in order to draw a small pistol if needed. In later feminist years, the female in film noir was viewed a bit more favorably, showing a strong woman who knew what she wanted, rather than being portrayed as a black widow spider, and what she wanted wasn't domesticity. Whether she was a good example for what women should be or not, she was bound to die in the end, having lured goodness knows how many men to their deaths on the way.

Films noir were often set at twilight or the early hours of the morning when God-fearing citizens were abed. The weather was always rainy and images of endless shots of rain pouring down cobbled alleyways was the norm. The settings were sordid—greasy spoons, bars, dance halls. When commentators speak of the setting of films noir, they often use the term "the sad city"—an uncaring, oppressive, and alienating place, making the city itself into one of the depressing characters.

Odd angles showed up in films noir, as if the photographer had had one too many. Shots were often taken from the ground up so that the character and the ceiling appeared together. Shots were harsh and angular and contrasted the sharp light, say from a sordid restaurant, onto a darkened street—scenes right out of Edward Hopper paintings. The lighting expressed the psychology of the

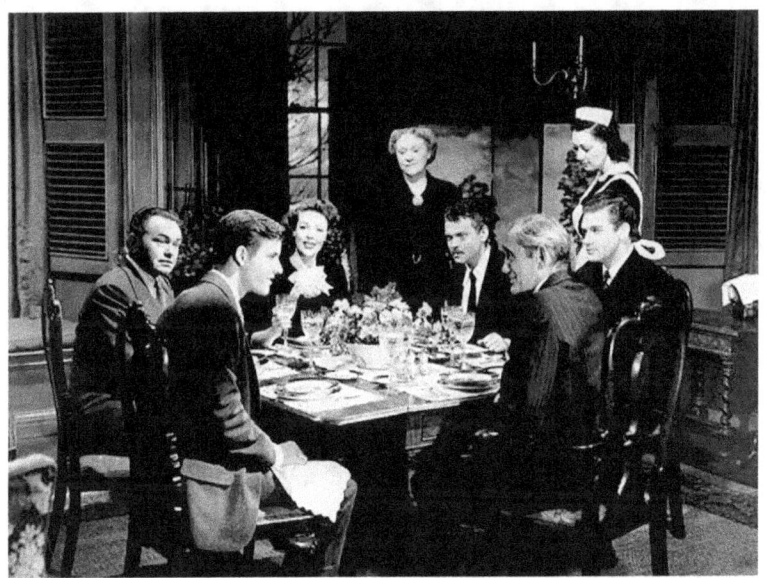

[left to right] Richard Long, Edward G. Robinson, Loretta Young, Martha Wentworth, Orson Welles, Philip Merivale, Byron Keith, and unknown actress in *The Stranger*, 1946

scene. World War II contributed much to the camera man's art both in film quality and the camera's technical capabilities, and this showed. Films noir were filled with moments when shadows from Venetian blinds were cast upon a body lying on the floor or with images of the protagonist's reflection seen in mirrors.

Where did these sordid, wretched, but compelling films come from? The writers for films noir were of the Mickey Spillane, Dashiell Hammett, Raymond Chandler school, with the clipped dialogue of Hemingway and a storyline carried forward by a monotone voice-over. Their directors were men who had left the shambles of a Europe sinking under the Nazis or who had returned from the war with its horrors firmly implanted in their psyches; with such a background, the American dream seemed futile. Nicholas Christopher said it was "as if the war, and the social eruptions in its aftermath, unleashed demons that had been bottled up in the national psyche." Film noir came from the raw evolutionary survivalist behaviors of male violence and female seductiveness, which, during the war, were often the reality. The hunger of the masses and the greed of the manipulators of the Great Depression also still hung around to add to all this disenchantment. The quality of "courage," which Hollywood had been promoting during the war, became a myth after the war; the happy family was an unreasonable goal. The anti-hero with his isolation, anxiety, and a general feeling of futility—this was closer to the ex-GI's frame of mind.

Film noir presented the opportunity for the loser to have a mystique; driven to disaster by Fate, we admired them while also fearing their raw energies. Film noir was a human response to the chaos of life and the loss of all one had once valued. As one character in *Detour* said, "Whichever way you turn, fate sticks out a foot to trip you." Film noir was about disillusionment and, in a strange way, martyrdom, the flawed hero, the ordinary person plunged into extraordinary circumstances. Even our favorite detectives only achieved a partial victory most times. These films declared the criminal justice system corrupt, the federal government oppressive, the daily office job dull, and the family unit a thing of the past—marriage was not a happy ending in most of them.

Detour was one of the great films noir. Add to that your own favorite—*The Maltese Falcon, The Third Man, The Postman Always Rings Twice, Double Indemnity, Notorious, This Gun for Hire*. And the stars of all this cynicism? Bogart and Bacall, Robert Mitchum, Orson Welles, Glen Ford, Richard Widmark, Veronica Lake, Jane Greer, Gloria Grahame, Ava Gardner, Barbara Stanwyck. And their characters stayed with us long after the plot had been forgotten.

What is it with these miserable films noir—as well as detective stories and true-life crime stories—that compel reasonable, ordinary, and law-abiding citizens to watch and read them? It is said we are fascinated by what we fear, and it's true the destruction of values and the general instability of all we hold good pervade these genres and cause us to shiver with the possibilities of our own lives being turned upside down by a wrongful accusation, by a twist

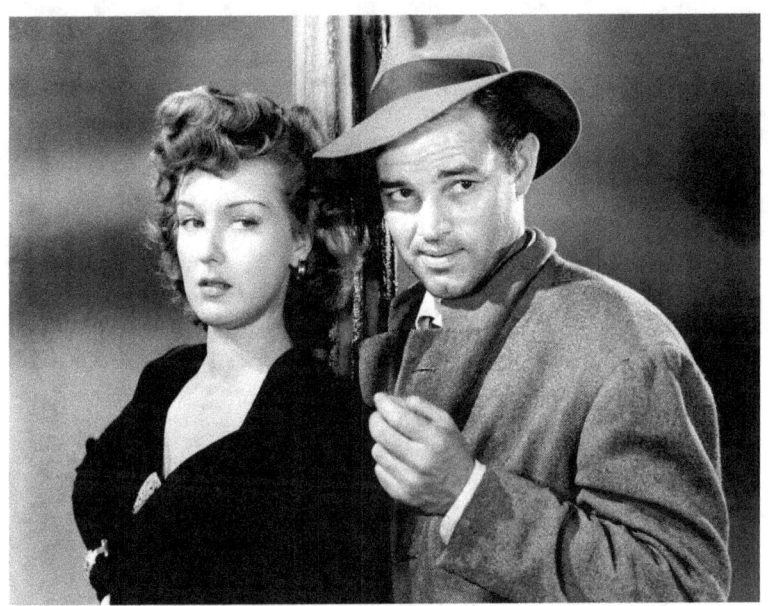

Ann Savage and Tom Neal in *Detour*, 1945

of fate. Like children screaming on a circus ride, film noir pushes us to the edge of possibilities, and teetering on the edge makes us return to our fairly mundane daily lives with a bit of relief and acceptance.

As the film critic Roger Ebert said, film noir was "the most American film genre because no society could have created a world so filled with doom, fate, fear, and betrayal, unless it were essentially naive and optimistic." Only an optimistic people could be that pessimistic.

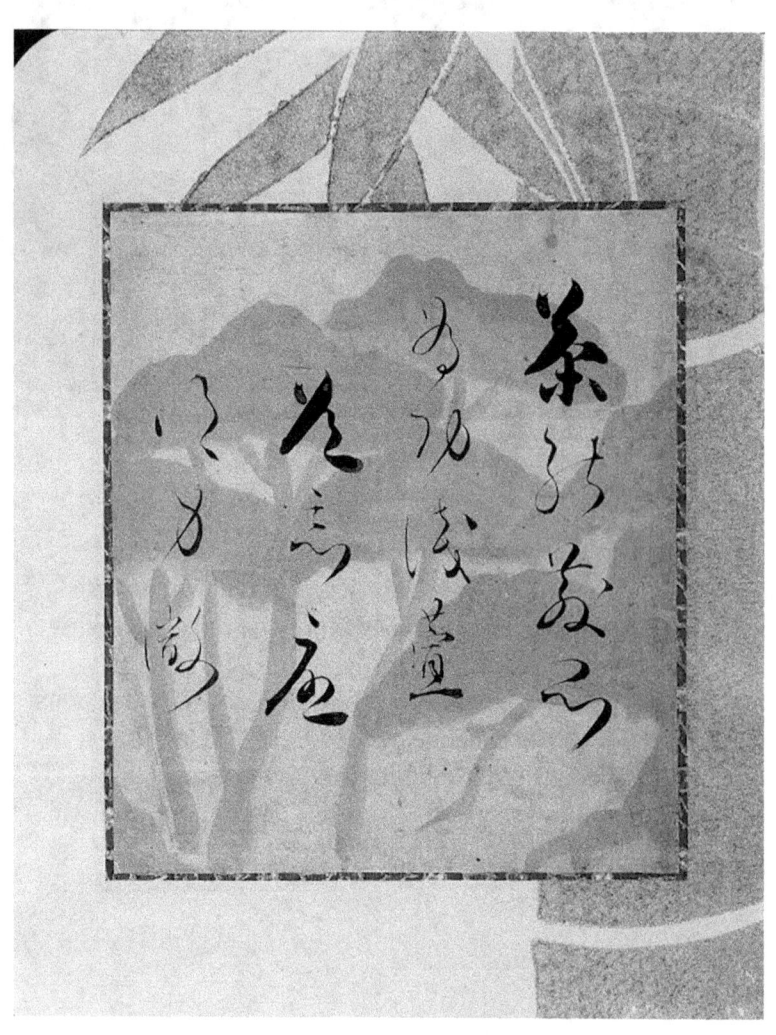

Honami Kōetsu and Tawaraya Sôtatsu, seventeenth century

the art of
calligraphy

I HAVE ALWAYS LOVED THE IMAGE OF BLACK INK
pouring out on paper. I was a skilled penman in the days when
penmanship counted—a rather long time ago. So it was natural
that when living in Japan, I should be drawn to the art of
Japanese calligraphy.

In traditional culture, Japanese literature and Japanese
calligraphy are closely interwoven since they are both done
with a brush, the actual writing (as distinct from the content
of the writing) being an art in itself. Within the brushstrokes
can be read the artist's "voice," that is, their emotions at
the time of doing the work and, indeed, almost their entire
approach to life. The twentieth-century Japanese artist Kazuo
Shiraga gives a beautiful description of this: "The first thing
that a man must do is grasp the material that is his from his
birth. This material explicates the difference between him
and other individuals through experienced sensation, spoken
words, paintings, sonority, and whatever else he may express.
He must therefore create a way to feel, speak and paint that is
his alone."

Sonja Arntzen, professor emerita, University of Toronto,
says, "The ancient and the modern exist together in
calligraphy as a contemporary art . . . as the new has been
added or created, the traditional has been transformed rather
than discarded." She points out the interesting difference
that currently exists between calligraphy as it is practiced in
the west and its practice in Japan. In the west—the scene of

extreme individual creative expression—calligraphy is self-effacing, as the calligrapher holds strictly to form. In Japan, however, where the self is never pushed forward in social life, advanced calligraphy is overflowing with the calligrapher's personality. There, the brushstroke is intended to reflect the human condition of the calligrapher at the moment of application.

But Japanese calligraphy goes deeper than just expressing "the self" on paper. Arntzen speaks of the *kotodama*, "the soul of words." She describes how "words are not just a means of describing what we experience, but they have a being of their own that can affect reality." She also accentuates that such self-expression is not egocentric, but has stretched beyond the ego to link to a universal wonderment. She quotes

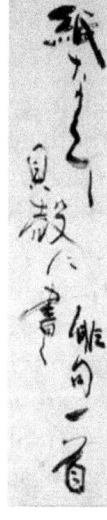

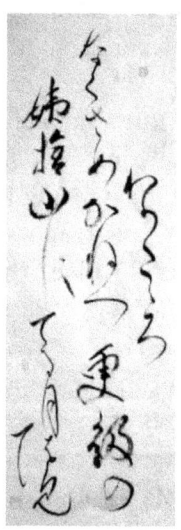

no paper
I write a haiku
on a shell

---

calligraphy by
Shikō Kataoka of
a haiku by Naomi
Beth Wakan

My heart
Is inconsolable
Seeing over Sarashima's
Old Forsaken Woman peak
The shining moon.

---

calligraphy by Sonja Arntzen
of "Foundation," a poem from
the Kokinshū anthology

calligrapher Iidaka Kazuko, "The moment one resolves to drop the first stroke onto the paper, living in this cosmic space, one entrusts to the brush the awe and joy of being graced with life."

Most Japanese calligraphers speak of a deep surge, a burning feeling that compels them to put brush to paper. Hokumei Nakano describes it this way: "When, as though I have been violently struck, I come into contact with a grave and powerful force that presses in on me, I feel something well up passionately within myself." Japanese calligraphers report not being able to contain the force and how it has to be harnessed. Hiroaki Toyama says it is like a "radiance of life well forth from within." And Taikō Yamamoto adds, "I feel I engrave myself into the paper." Seikaku Takagi puts it this way, "Strength and exhilaration within confinement." *Shodō*, the way of the brush, is a welling of emotion that, if the calligrapher steps out of the way, will control the brush.

The ink for Japanese calligraphy is not a liquid. It is a stick of vegetable soot and glue that has been compressed together. The best ink uses fine soot and only a small amount of glue so that the stick is of the same consistency throughout. The calligrapher grinds the stick (*sumi*) on a special ink-stone (*suzuri*) using a small amount of water kept in a special container (*mizusashi*). Although bottled ink can now be purchased, no one but a beginner would ever think of not grinding their own ink. In addition, the ink has to be just the right consistency to fit the emotion being expressed. If the ink is too thick it won't run down the page and if too thin it will trickle everywhere and won't be easy to control. It is as if the inkstick has a life of its own for which the calligrapher must make allowances. The making of the ink alone is a meditation, even before one has made the first stroke. Although inks come in many colors these days, traditional black still dominates.

The paper used for calligraphy is washi, a type of paper made in Japan from the fibers of certain kinds of tree bark. Washi is much stronger than paper made from wood pulp. The washi is placed on some black felt (*shitajiki*) and kept in position with a weight (*bunchin*). The color and pattern on the paper is chosen carefully to match the words. Sometimes calligraphy is done on silk.

The calligraphy brush (*fude*) is made by craftsmen using a variety of types of hairs—sheep, dog, cat, rabbit, or horse. Calligraphers choose their brushes carefully because different types of hairs behave differently with ink; some are very absorbent while others release ink more easily.

Once ink is applied to paper, the size and thickness of the stroke is very important. The line must flow from the top to the bottom of the page with the required variations of paleness and thickness. The calligrapher gets the desired effect by applying or reducing pressure on the brush and, of course, making the ink the right consistency. The space around the calligraphy is important also, since negative space is just as important as positive space for the Japanese.

In contrast to the often stark black and white of the calligraphy and paper, Japanese calligraphers sign their work with a chop, a seal carved with the calligrapher's identity. The chop is generally imprinted with red ink.

Modest-sized pieces of calligraphy are made in kneeling position (buttocks on the heels), but for larger pieces the calligrapher stands and bends down to the paper resting on the floor. As strokes are made, the feet have their own choreography that is enchanting to watch.

There are three main types of Japanese calligraphy—*Kaisho*, *Gyōsho*, and *Sōsho*. *Kaisho* (meaning correct writing) strokes are closest to being clearly defined so that the writing can be easily read. Students begin with this style while they are getting used to handling the brush. The brush is lifted from the paper after each stroke. *Gyōsho* (travel writing) is cursive writing where the strokes flow together in a more rounded style, similar to what we know as handwriting. In *Sōsho* (grass writing) the brush doesn't leave the paper as the flowing form takes dominance over the legibility. Sometimes strokes are eliminated entirely in order to obtain an attractive flow.

Classical Japanese calligraphy uses the Chinese writing system or syllabary (*kanji*) or an adaptation of it. Chinese writing, introduced into Japan about 600 C.E., was the basis for all subsequent Japanese writing systems. A few hundred years later, *kana*, an abbreviated form of the Chinese symbols, began to be used for the vernacular. This form was mainly used by women who were not thought capable of learning the complex Chinese *kanji*. It was during the years of the Heian period (794–1185 C.E.) that the Japanese really started to develop a style of calligraphy that became their own, as distinct from that borrowed from the Chinese. Schools of calligraphy such as the Sesonji and Shōren were founded. Even today, this ancient form of *kana* is used in calligraphy.

Modern writing uses a mixture of *kana* and *kanji* in modified form with *katakana* (meaning fragmentary *kana*) in use for foreign words.

If only one or two *kanji* symbols are used in a calligraphy piece, often they will be abbreviated to almost abstract form.

Sometimes calligraphy uses abstract forms with no connection at all to *kana* or *kanji*. Certainly, Japanese calligraphy since 1945 is more about form than meaning as the *zen-ei sho* (avant-garde) style came into favor.

The entire completed piece of calligraphy is appreciated visually as a work of art long before it is read. *Shodō* is much like a piece of abstract art in that it is deeply emotional and also has a meaningful poem embedded in it.

The practice of Japanese calligraphy was much influenced by Zen thought. For any single piece, the calligrapher has but one chance. Strokes cannot be corrected. Calligraphy is practiced by Buddhist monks because, to write masterfully, one must clear the mind and let the letters flow. Calligraphers must be able to focus, but in a relaxed way; tremendous effort will not necessarily produce good work. As in other Japanese art forms, the calligrapher is expected to "get out of the way."

Having Japanese calligraphy pieces in your home can be a form of meditation as their beauty can be uplifting, and the emotions they invoke can be cathartic when contemplated.

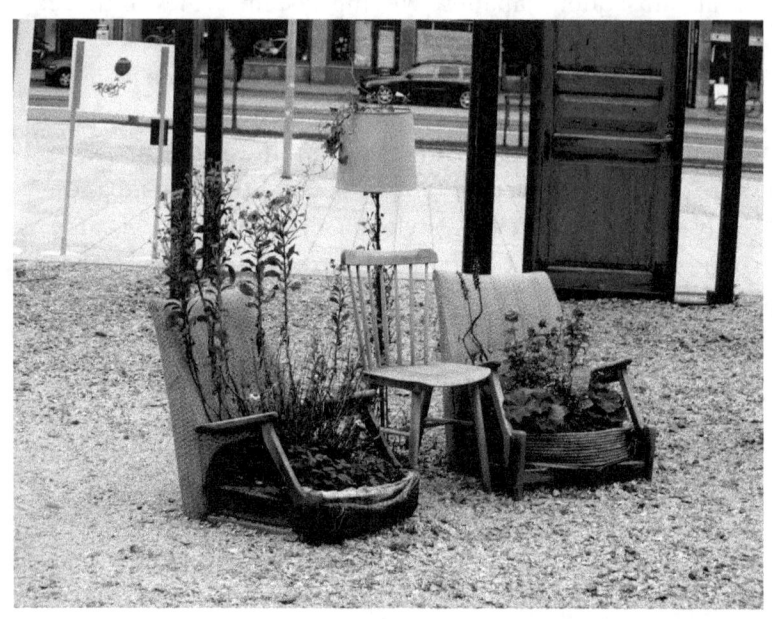

Chixoy, *Furniture as Planters*, 2008

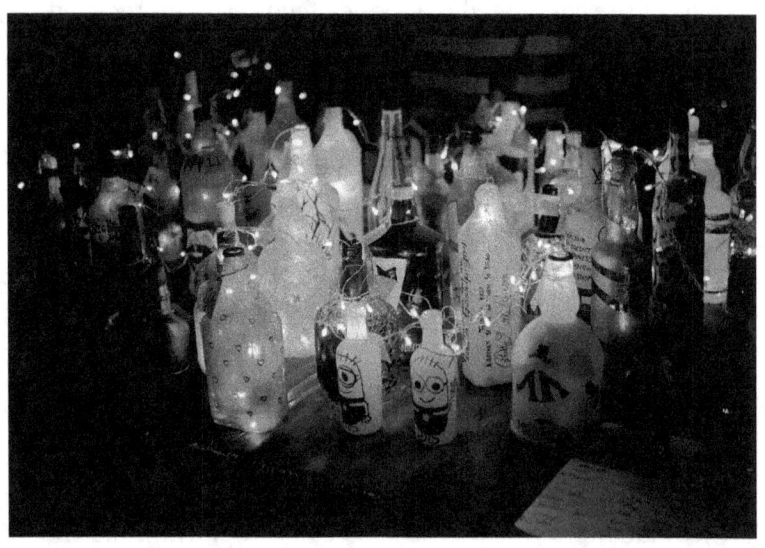

Prakhar Chaudhary, *Throw Them Away or Make Magic*, 2015

the art of
recycling

I HAVE NOT BOUGHT A NEW PIECE OF CLOTHING, WITH
the exception of shoes and underwear, for over twenty years.
Not only is my wardrobe made up of cast-offs, but a lot of the
furnishings in our house came from other people's reckless
purchasing and subsequent discarding when they got bored
with their purchases. I do not tell this in a self-righteous
manner but with the satisfactory glow I have when I look
around our home at all the orphans we have given shelter to,
everything from a quilt I made from other women's knitting
projects that they tired of, to a discarded medical bedside table
converted to a dictionary stand.

It seems obvious then that art using discarded material
would attract my attention. Particularly, I like artists who
assemble found objects. On the top of our bedroom chest
of drawers is a very nice little assemblage that I made
myself (p. 152). The base is a very neat and conventional
piece of quilting, reminding me I have never been either
neat or conventional. On the left is a large brain coral
obtained long ago from a museum being down-sized, which
represents my constant exploration of what consciousness
might be. On the right are the remains of some flower
in a small discarded Japanese saké wine cup, and a bowl
matching the pattern of the pashmina scarf on the wall;
this scarf has been stretched over an old painting frame
and given its own little shelf. At night my husband adds his
wallet to the arrangement and I, my reading glasses. That

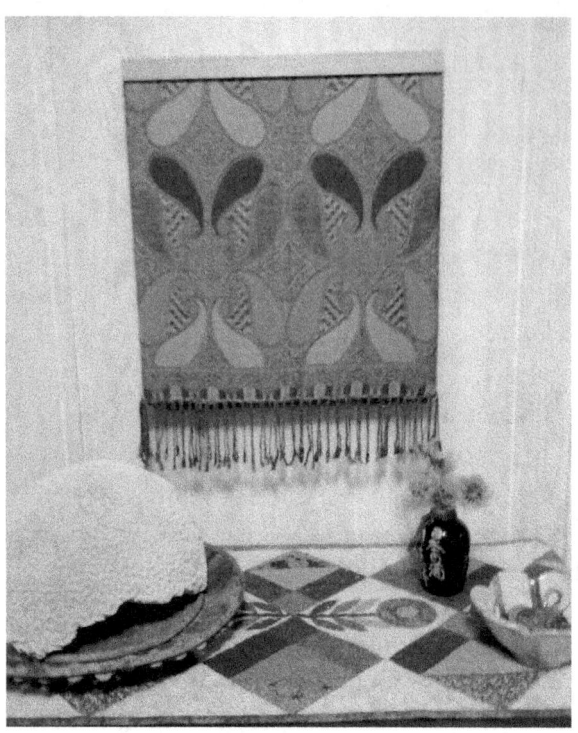

An assemblage made by Naomi

display of found objects rarely gets seen by an audience
other than ourselves, and yet, as an example of discards
made into art, it is really most satisfactory. The texture
and palette of these objects are all things that appeal to
my husband and me. They perhaps also have an element of
sentimental attachment; they bring back memories.

Ever since Duchamp put an old bicycle wheel and kitchen
stool together to use as possibly the first kinetic sculpture,
artists have been looking to the trash of our culture to
convert it into art. Sometimes they do this to make a political
statement about the "purchasing culture" that ours has
become. Lea Vergine, the art critic, declared that "to save
and preserve trash, to try to hold onto it, to help it to survive
by rescuing it from the void, from nothingness, from the
dissolution to which it is destined, the desire to leave a trace,
a sign, a hint for posterity, involves a psychological dimension
that is also political." An example of environmental concern

is Inguna Gremzde who did amazing little paintings inside bottle caps. The artist's statement of these is: "My current practice explores the human and nature relationship. In my artwork, I examine different possibilities in interpretation of human alienation from nature by hinting at consumer lifestyle as a probable reason."

Other times artists retrieve and recycle for the practical reason that such material is all they can afford to work with. Albert Einstein may have said, "People love chopping wood. In this activity one immediately sees results." But how about people who don't chop wood but prefer putting wood pieces together, building up structures that, while not producing body-warming wood for the stove, produce heart-and-spirit-warming structures that can transport one to the far limits of the imagination. Sound exaggerated?

Louise Nevelson, that icon and influential sculptor of the mid-twentieth century, recreated herself as she recreated the junk wood she collected. Her personal stories—of her father's wood connection as a dealer in lumber and as a one-time woodcutter, her Jewish immigration, her unsuccessful marriage to a wealthy man, the struggles of becoming an influential and accepted woman artist—are all reflected in her work. Just as she melded the cast-off bits of wood she gathered into monumental pieces by using monochrome paint, so she made her own personality, the bits of her life, larger than life by melding them into a publicly recognizable figure. Nevelson's larger-than-life life was shown in her wooden pieces, which were a metaphor for, as she put it, "the self of me."

She denied all labels that were attached to her from time to time, such as Jewess, mother, feminist, surrealist. She was an artist who just happened to be born Jewish, had acquired a son, and was a woman. She never denied, however, that her pieces were almost always self-portraits. Of *The Bride of the Black Moon*, she said, "It's me, of course." Her failed marriage had to be the basis for her room-sized environments on the theme, such as *Dawn's Wedding Chapel*.

Of her pieces as metaphor, she equated black to night and

the passage of the hours of the day, white to early morning and emotional promise, and gold to royalty and riches. Death became personified in her monumental pieces on the Holocaust. All black rooms, all white rooms, all gold rooms—she made the waste of society into glorious installations that one's psyche could enter and recreate for oneself.

Nevelson worked with a limited palette, perhaps influenced by her teacher Hans Hofmann, who advocated the discipline of his students working within limitations. Although at the beginning and at the end of her career, she worked with bronze and other metals, her signature material was found wooden objects. She described her work in this way: "It is really additive. You add and add and add." And what she added were banister parts, bits of baseball bats, toilet seats, parts of chairs, molding, knobs, dowels . . . and she made the additions into a sum by the use of one-color paint. Somehow, the past of the bits she gathered together was obliterated in the black, or white, or gold paint that made them a complete piece of art. She was also very much influenced by Picasso, who, she said, "gave us structure."

As I have included her here as an artist who worked with found material, I should mention that, although her earlier pieces were almost entirely made up of found objects, her later pieces were assembled from wood cut in the studio and were much sleeker, and, for me, less appealing.

As I like boundaries, I am very fond of trash that has been gathered and arranged within a box, within a frame. It is as if the fresh setting shows the articles in a new light. I appreciate Joseph Cornell's and Alison Knowles's boxes in this respect. I also like piles of things, so Pistoletto's stack of rag-covered bricks with a shoe on top I find most appealing. If a large number of any object is gathered together, the object takes on a novel import, a new meaning, such as when Kounellis arranged bottles on a piece of plywood; Agullo gathered different-sized shoe taps and patterned them on wood in his piece *Étude d'un lieu*; and Rheinsberg did an installation of hundreds of found shoes and gloves.

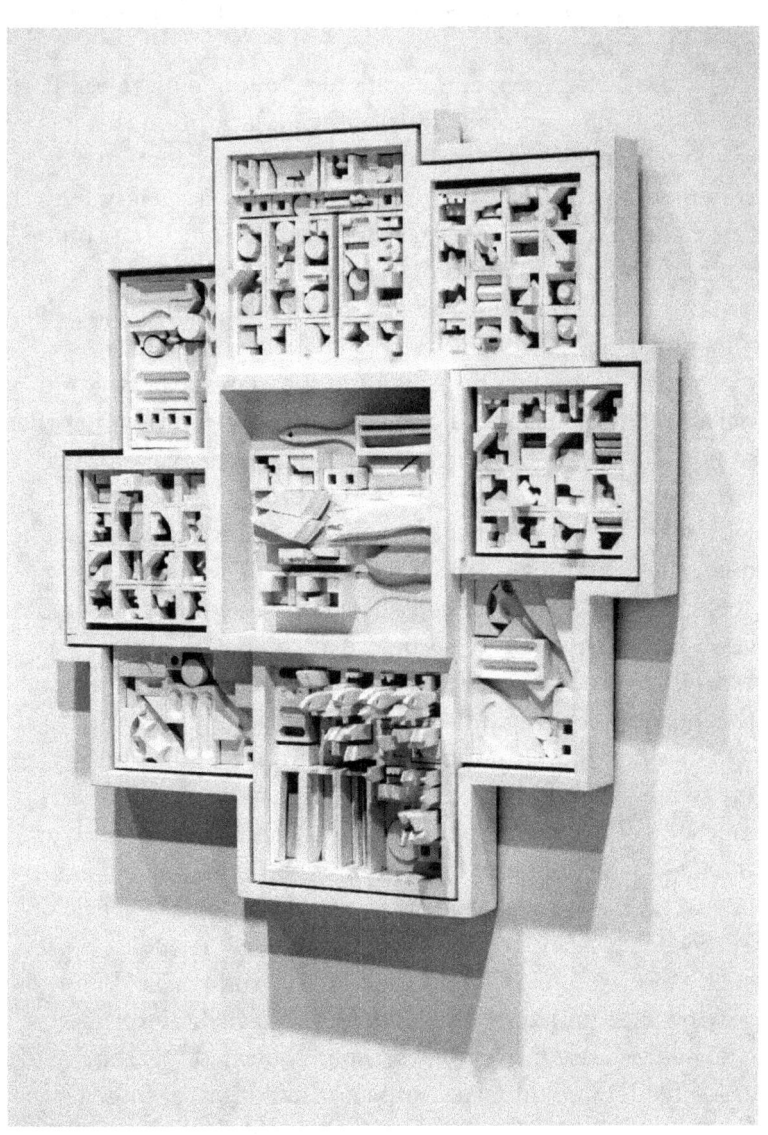

Louise Nevelson, *Dawn's Landscape*, 1975

Found art is rarely beautiful in the traditional sense, though I find Spoerri's arrangement of objects on panels (his snares), to be quite wonderfully attractive. But many of these artists, using our society's throw-aways, are aiming at things other than beauty.

Picasso, when he made a bull's head out of a bicycle seat and handlebars, was caught up in the juxtaposition that presented novelty, rather than making an environmental statement. The artist César viewed trash not as society's rejects but as "useful material that someone left lying around." Rauschenberg similarly said, "A pair of socks is no less suitable to make a painting with than wood, nails, turpentine, oil, and fabric." Kurt Schwitters, that master of collage, explained, "It matters little whether the materials employed have already been shaped or formed for some purpose or other, or not. The wheel from a baby carriage, metal chicken wire, twine, and cotton balls are all elements on an equal standing with pigment. Artists create by selecting, starting over and deforming their materials." Sculptor, Alik Cavaliere, when speaking of the process, said, "The first violent and inevitable clash with a new reality has been overcome with a purely escapist approach: the art of chance, of welter, of discards, of the old, and of trash, followed by the elevation of detritus to a mythical status." Moholy-Nagy described how "during my strolls, I would gather used machine parts, screws, bolts, mechanical parts. I placed them on wooden boards, applying them with glue or nails, and I combined them with elements of painting." No revolutionary statement here, just a curiosity as to what aesthetic effect could be achieved. Actually, artists such as Picasso and Niki de Saint Phalle could be said to be playing with junk, just for the sheer joy of their cleverness.

The trash used in artworks can be squashed together, assembled, piled up, made into an installation, arranged into images, pulverized, compressed . . . it's all material for creativity. Some artists, such as César or Spoerri, worked only with discards. Others have just used them at certain phases of their work, such as Beuys's artistic period of his sleighs filled with animal fat and fur.

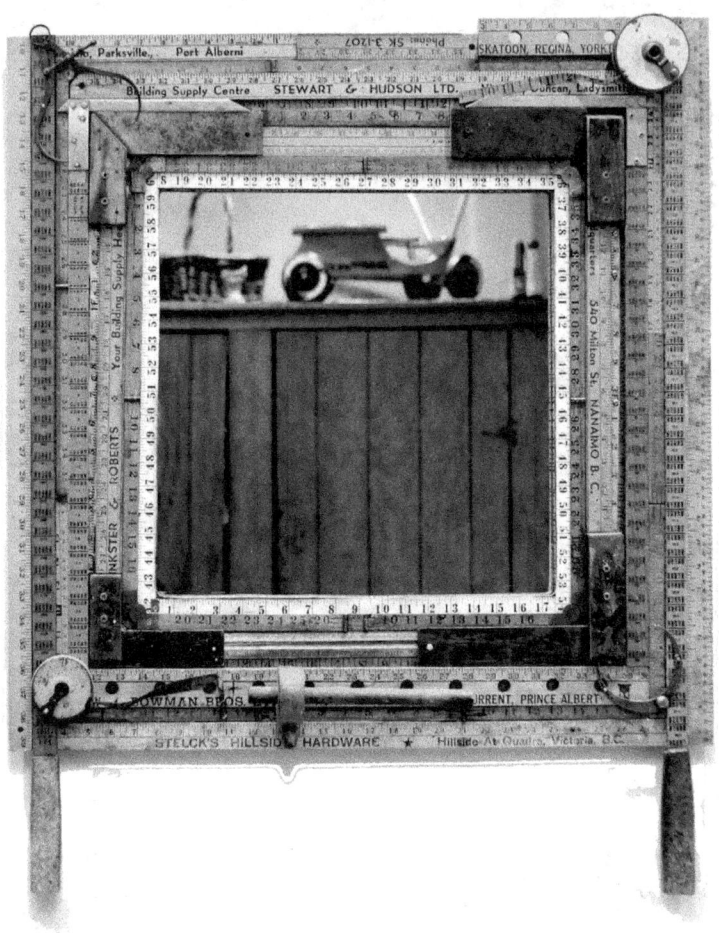

Chris Straw, *Mirror Framed with Antique Rulers*

The recycling of trash for artistic purposes seems to me a valid and exciting thing to do, "an embracement of the abandoned," as Anthony Julius phrased it. This embracement not only reflects my own tendency in my creative works to "weave straw into gold," but it also proves that not all folk sayings are correct, and that you actually can make a silk purse out of a sow's ear.

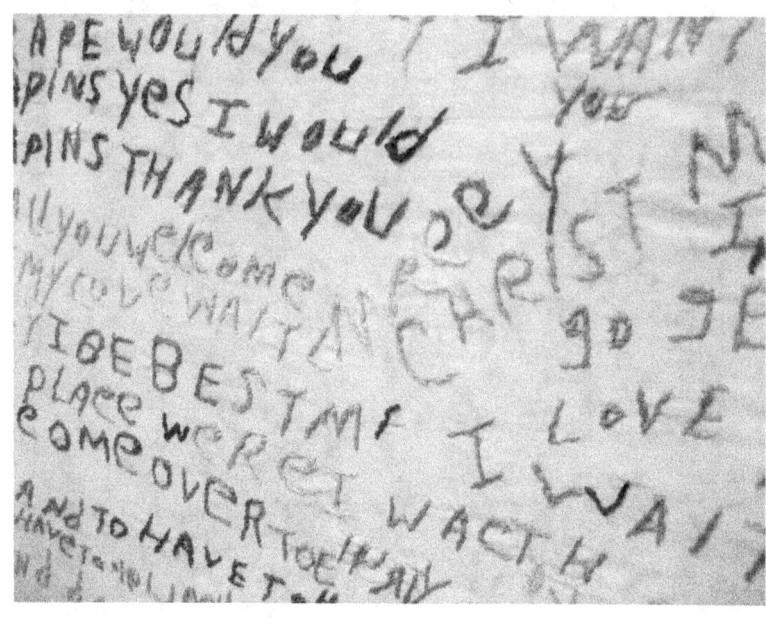

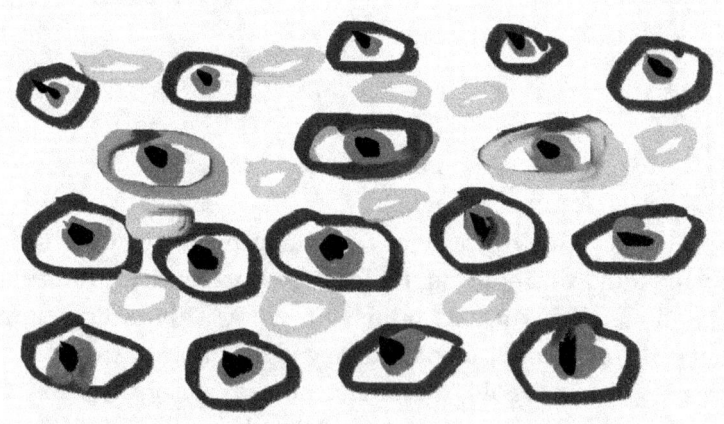

Art made by institutionalized patients with schizophrenia

the art of
outsiders

"IT TAKES ONE TO KNOW ONE" IS A CLICHÉ, BUT USEFUL in this case: as a person who has always perched cheerfully on the margin of life, I think I am qualified, to a small extent, to write about artists working at the edge of society, or even beyond the edge. Many artists are anti-social to some extent, their creativity springing from a certain dissatisfaction with life. Creativity comes from not being satisfied with things the way they are—the more dissatisfied, possibly the more creative the artist.

The Outsider Artists that I want to speak of in this chapter are not so much dissatisfied as marginalized. Artists are expected to be unusual, novel, but if they go too far outside expected societal limits, they are labeled "mad" and their work is no longer thought of as art. Ernst Kris, the psychoanalyst, points out that "Art is controlled madness. The artist goes into unknown territory and returns." Michel Thévoy, the art historian, described this process so well: "The artist inoculates himself with the disease the better to neutralize it. That is, art is his/her mental hygiene." First there is unease, then there is inattention (unconscious scanning), then the work is created, and then the ego returns. The Art Brut artists I want to write about here don't return. They cut themselves free from anchors.

Art Brut, translated as "raw art," is a term that covers Outsider Art and was first defined by Jean Dubuffet in this way: "Those works created from solitude, and from pure and authentic creative impulses—where the worries of competition, acclaim and social promotion do not interfere—are, because of these very facts, more precious than the productions of professionals. After a certain familiarity with these flourishings of an exalted feverishness, lived so fully and so intensely by their authors, we cannot avoid the feeling that in relation to these works, cultural art in its entirety appears to be the game of a futile society, a fallacious parade." Dubuffet put Art Brut on a pedestal as a goal for all true artists when he said, "The madman is a reformer, an inventor of new systems, intoxicated with invention. . . . This is exactly what is required of the artist, and explains why the creation of art is so worthless when it does not originate in a state of alienation, when it fails to offer a new conception of the world and new principles for living."

Dubuffet was saying, I think, that the mainstream art "culture" manages to absorb every new approach in art and, by doing so, makes it impotent, takes out its sting of freshness. Art Brut, on the other hand, withstands this onslaught because artists who might be defined as Art Brut (many of them mentally disturbed in various ways and some of them actually living in institutions) aren't interested in the marketing and commercializing of their art into the mainstream. As John M. MacGregor, author of *The Discovery of the Art of the Insane*, wrote, "Dubuffet attacked 'the vast apparatus of professionals—critics, historians, educators, curators, dealers, and artists.'"

I should mention as an aside here that these days, because drugs are provided for psychoses, much current art made in mental hospitals is flattened, dull, and lacking in any kind of originality. For this reason, the market in Art Brut artists of earlier years is much in demand and often runs into the six figures. (That's what I mean by dumbing it down by using fresh art as an investment product.)

Even the most isolated of Outsider Artists still paint within the culture that he/she was brought up in, and that may show in the subject matter and colors chosen in the execution of their pieces. Still, it is the inner drive and the inner vision that sets them apart. Outsider Artists can create within the boundaries of accepted art but be outside the regular art market, or can create outside the conventional boundaries of what might be considered art. Yet, either way, intensity of purpose is present in all they do.

Many of these people, who are roughly clumped together under the title "Outsider Artists," have at one time or another been picked up and exploited commercially. There are actually galleries (not necessarily exploitive) devoted to this kind of art, such as Intuit: The Center for Intuitive and Outsider Art in Chicago and the American Visionary Art Museum in Baltimore, Maryland. Some visionary art is more like an installation or outdoor construction, such as *Watts Towers* by Simon Rodia, *Buddha Park* and *Sala Keoku* by Bunleua Sulilat, *The Palais Ideal* by Ferdinand Cheval (which took thirty years to construct and started from a pebble he picked up on his mailman rounds), and Nek Chand's *Rock Garden at Chandigarh*.

A teacher once told me that schizophrenics were just an inch away from the truth. I never quite knew what he meant. He certainly wasn't romanticizing that terrible brain disorder, yet what might he have been telling me? Perhaps he was suggesting that if one's brain wiring was not as the average, a person can connect things in unusual ways, unusual ways that could hint at what the universe might be about. Prinzhorn, the psychotherapist and art historian who was an early collector of the art of mentally disturbed people, believed that their art came from deep in the psyche, and he also thought these people were in some way privileged to have access to ultimate truths. He didn't view their art from a pathological viewpoint. He felt his patients' art illustrated the mechanism of true creativity. It is important to note, however, that Prinzhorn and others who worked in institutions and collected Outsider Art carefully selected the works they spoke about, which therefore didn't really represent the total artistic output of mental institutions at that time. Robert Hughes, the art critic, comments that "Romanticism's core was the idea that mental derangement gave access to a whole 'dark' side of the mind, the locus of painful, but irrefutable truths about society, human nature and especially art." It was wrong, of course, for not all "mad" people produce art of a high level, just as not all "sane" people can. Many conventional artists, such as William Kurelek, were also confined to mental hospitals from time to time and, to a certain extent, could be considered "Outsider" artists.

To clarify things for myself and for the reader, I'd like to list some generalizations about the outlier artists' approach to their creations. These generalizations are just that, and they may apply to some and not to others, but still these qualities seem prevalent in Outsider Artists:

- Outsider Artists tend to express things directly.

- Outsider Artists tend to be self-taught, not hindered by art training, and they ignore the expectations of the "high" art community.

- Outsider Artists are not interested in communication, but pursue their own path intently. There is no devious desire to please the public, no thought of an audience, no ambition, for they are driven by a need to give order to their lives and not to earn a living or get outside approval. Their work is closer to a monologue than a dialogue.

- Outsider Artists have the innocence of children but their strokes have the assurance children's art can never have.

- Outsider Artists like to fill their canvases, either with writing or with smaller and smaller images of the main image. They often use repetition and avoid blank spaces. They seem to work from an obsessional inner drive. As Francesco Bonami, the Italian art curator, put it, "Insider artists know how to frame their compulsions. Outsiders cannot stop." They are also confident of their means of expression, however unskilled.

- This ordered life their art seeks often takes the form of higher realms, which they can enter at will and almost live a parallel life there. As Roger Cardinal, the author of *Outsider Art*, so well put it, "they are exploring the psychic elsewhere."

- The imaginary worlds created by Outsider Artists are often developed over a long period of time, building their oeuvre up over many years, sometimes only finishing with their deaths.

- Outsider Artists are usually excluded, not only from the mainstream of art, but from the mainstream of the culture they live within; they are marginalized by economic status, immigrant status, education, or pathology.

- Often the talents of Outsider Artists appear in later life. Old age does seem to be a perfect time to be creative in a way one never could have before, since one possibly no longer cares about social success.

- While many Outsider Artists claim to not know where their inspiration comes from, the mediumistic Outsider Artists claim to be only a conduit of higher powers.

- Outsider Artists tend to use non-artistic materials or at least mix their media, not from any artistic concern but mainly because it is readily available and cheap—discarded clothing, paper, and metal scraps. This is because many Art Brut artists come from backgrounds of extreme poverty.

- Conventional artists fit into a history; even if they break laws, their breakthroughs become new laws. Art Brut artists can't be put chronologically into any order. They do not influence each other.

- Outsider Artists often abandon their living space to their creations, covering walls with visions from their alternate lives.

Max Ernst, Sophie Taeuber-Arp, Pablo Picasso, Paul Klee, and the Surrealists all looked to Outsider Art to reinvigorate themselves, and they treated the work of the institutionalized as genuine art because of the exposure to it provided by Prinzhorn. I should mention here that artists had long been looking for new influences to reinvigorate Western art. In the late nineteenth century, Chinese and Japanese art opened the eyes of many artists, such as Pierre Bonnard, Henri de Toulouse-Lautrec, Mary Cassatt, Edgar Degas, Pierre-Auguste Renoir, Claude Monet, Vincent van Gogh, Camille Pissarro, and Paul Gauguin. Colonialism had also introduced the artwork of tribal peoples. African art particularly had compelling effects on artists such as Picasso and Henri Matisse. While "colonial" art was considered fascinating, it just appeared "freer" because it was different. It should not be confused with Art Brut.

Opening to the art of other cultures, however, made the shift to highly valuing the art of Outsiders inevitable. The Surrealists particularly tended to romanticize the purity and naivety of the direct art of the Outsider, forgetting the morbid pathology that accompanied most of it. The Surrealists, who placed extraordinary emphasis on the value of the unconscious in the artistic process, were quite naturally drawn to the art of the institutionalized where obsession overrode conscious choice.

Probably the best known Outsider Artist is Henry Darger, who was a recluse. It is thought he may have had Asperger syndrome. Over the years, he produced a 15,145-page fantasy work consisting of thirteen densely typed volumes, eighty-seven large watercolor murals, and hundreds of drawings. The titles alone told so much about his isolation and his pleas for the rights of children: *The Story of the Vivian Girls in What is Known as the Realms of the Unreal, of the Glandeco-Angellinian War Storm, Caused by the Child Slave Rebellion.*

Darger felt he could see through adults' lies and, even as a young boy, knew what a fraud the world was. He withdrew from it, supporting himself as a janitor. He lived in a room on Chicago's North Side, and for forty-three years produced his amazing oeuvre. His work much reflected his own unfortunate childhood and expounded the view that children had a right to be happy and unexploited. In his own words, "To play, to be happy, and to dream, the right to normal sleep of the night's season, the right to an education, that we may have an equality of opportunity for developing all that are in us of mind and heart." As you can see, he identified closely with the cause of children's rights.

It is ironic that the work of this recluse can be found in several major American museums and has been the feature of many exhibits. Although unintended, Darger had a marked influence on many other artists, not just for the morality and complexity of his writing and artwork, but also because of the years of driven dedication he gave to his art.

Adolf Wölfli was one of the earliest Outsider Artists whose work was taken seriously. His thousands of drawings were part of a fantasy life he invented for himself in which he became Saint Adolf. His early life was miserable; his alcoholic father deserted the family, and his mother died by the time Adolf was nine. Abusive foster parents and forced hard work on their farms brutalized him. Wölfli's fantasy world was drawn without first planning and had the characteristic of many institutionalized Outsider Artists, that of fully filling the page. Often he would collage advertisements or magazine illustrations into his work, but there was no intent to use them as political or social commentary. He thought that his art came from another source, as did many of the visionary and mediumistic artists. He felt that he himself could never have the imagination to create the wonderful worlds he painted.

The names of other Outsider Artists follow, each worth further study:

Felipe Jesus Consalvos worked in a cigar factory and used cigar bands and cigar papers for his more than eight hundred collages.

Martin Ramirez was institutionalized with schizophrenia and was a self-taught artist. He did over three hundred colored-pencil drawings, surrounding each image with concentric circles.

Charles Dellschau, a retired butcher, made thirteen books of drawings, paintings, and collages. He is interesting because all of his artwork was of airships and fantasy airships.

Among the Outsider Artists who did large constructions can be listed **James Hampton** who, like Darger, worked as a janitor.

Achilles Rizzoli, unlike the others, had formal art training and was employed as a draughtsman. It was only after his death that his drawings were found, many of which personify people as buildings. A film was made of these and of his life—*Yield to Total Elation: The Life and Art of Achilles Rizzoli.*

Bill Traylor, born into slavery and a sharecropper after emancipation, was such a typical example of the pattern of many Outsider Artists' lives. He first started drawing at the age of eighty-five in order to document his life experiences.

Charles Castle, a self-taught, profoundly deaf artist, used found materials, along with saliva and ink made from woodstove soot. He was entirely oblivious of the art world and, in fact, of life outside his small town. He never learned to speak, read, or write.

William Edmondson was a sculptor. He is an example of a visionary artist, for he said he had been commanded by God to become a sculptor.

Nek Chand Saini was one of the best known large-scale construction Outsider Artists. While working as a roads inspector, he recycled materials and built his imaginary kingdom of Sukrani in a gorge in

Chandigarh, India. He somehow managed to hide it during the eighteen years of its construction, by which time it stretched over eighteen acres. Pandit Nehru wanted Chandigarh to be an ideal city and employed the renowned architect Le Corbusier to design it. Chand was terrified that his work would be discovered and destroyed. He eventually showed it to the chief architect of Chandigarh, N. M. Sharma. Sharma was overwhelmed by it, but he also worried about its destruction should it be found since Chand's surreal people, animals, and shelters were right next to Le Corbusier's world-famous works. Sharma supported Chand, and eventually, in 1976, Chand's work was acknowledged and named *The Rock Garden,* and he was given the title Director-Creator. He was slotted as an environmental builder, but it is his intensity of purpose that makes him an Outsider, no matter what other labels are attached to him. Chand created a private world that today is open to the public and supported by the government.

Is Outsider Art a way of dealing with extreme adversity—poverty, marginalization, neurological damage, mental illness? Does Outsider Art provide a road map toward restoring balance for the artist? Rather than a representation of disease, is Outsider Art a kind of healing for the artist? Are Outside Artists to be wondered at rather than ridiculed or "treated?"

These Outsider Artists named above, I feel, were trying to come to terms with their own disordered lives, trying to make some sense of their visions, dreams, and nightmares. It's possible that what we call "normality" may be just us adapting to things as they are, capitulating to the reigning way of looking at things? Is it possible that "madness" is not an illness, but just a different way of viewing life?

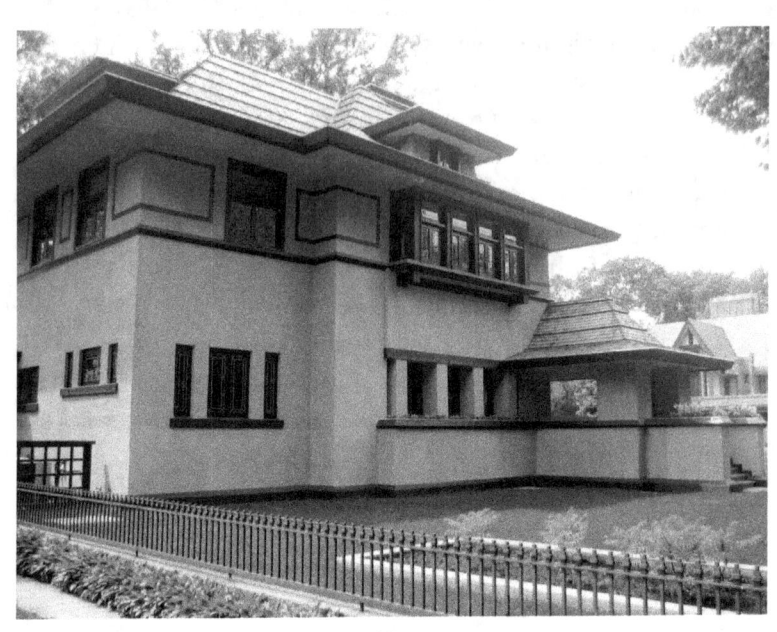

Frank Lloyd Wright, Edward R. Hills House, Oak Park, Illinois

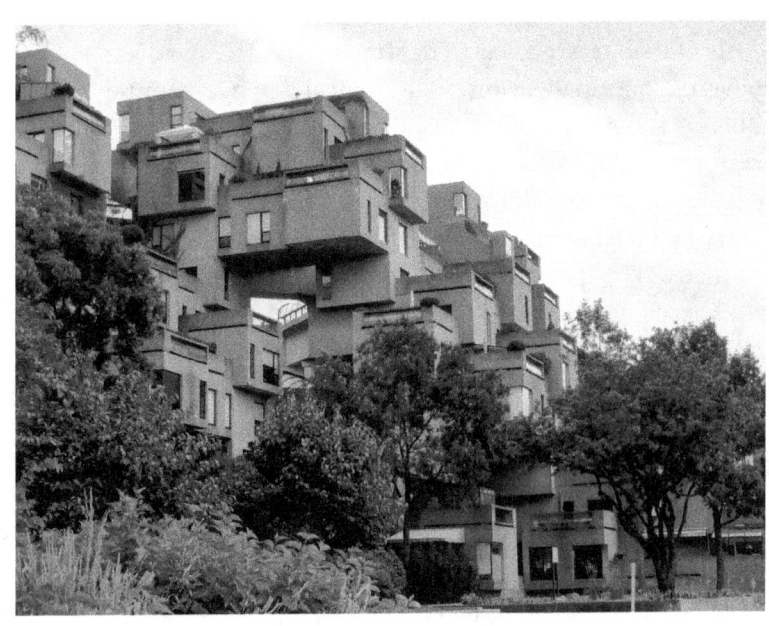

Moshe Safdie, Habitat 67, Montreal, Canada

the art of
happy architecture

Antoni Gaudí, the Spanish architect whose life began in the mid-nineteenth century and spilled into the first quarter of the twentieth, does not strike me as having been a happy man. He has recently been considered for sainthood, and such people rarely have happy lives, certainly not happy in the sense of everyday folks. Gaudí was unlucky in love and never married, though of course that does not necessarily equate with a recipe for misery. Millions have been moved by Gaudí's unfinished cathedral in Barcelona: La Sagrada Familia (The Holy Family). While I typically long for the simplicity of Corbusier, I strangely got hooked along the way by Gaudí's ornate and organic decorations for the houses he built for domestic use, albeit for the very wealthy.

Happiness doesn't have to be about challenging the gods with the sky-piercing buildings of Dubai and Singapore. Such proud and soaring buildings seem self-conscious and out of touch. Height and mass are piercing; horizontal is calming. I prefer buildings that define neighborhoods, with areas in which to be active and social, with benches and green spaces. I want public buildings that draw people downtown to the village core, the city center, with room enough for evening strolls.

Such preferences include "happy" buildings. What might be the qualities of buildings that make people happy and make them smile with delight when they see them? What architectural elements make people eager to return to their homes after a hard day's work?

Order, elegance, and balance are often listed as desirable elements in buildings. Certainly, order is a way of simplifying our lives, yet do we want to live in an "ordered" building, or even to visit one? Simple doesn't always win over complex, nor order over confusion. Yes, we would like our buildings to blend with nature and be made of healthy materials, but at the same time, we often demand that they be equipped with state-of-the-art technology to save our labors. I, for sure, would choose modesty over luxury, but that may not be what makes others happy. Nor may my desire to live in a recycled home please everyone; certainly it wouldn't please our local building inspector, whose building codes do not favor the re-use of lumber and old window frames.

A building must fulfill its function, of course, and in the case of a home, that means shelter and solidity. But we also want the home to go beyond basic needs and promise us happiness. A house is a sanctuary, but more, it affirms for us the values we aspire to. Certainly, when my husband and I consciously chose to live in an environment and house that would bring us happiness, we did so because of a commitment to contentment; that was one of the aims of our move. We wanted a home that exuded friendliness, intelligence, kindness, and generosity. We wanted our home to remind us that we're OK. We wanted a space where we would feel free to fulfill our potential. We wanted a home where we would feel "at home" with ourselves. That is, our wished-for house was one that would allow us to be the best versions of ourselves.

We eventually settled on Gabriola Island near Vancouver, Canada, in a little vinyl-sided cottage. Country cottages speak of Eden before the expulsion. We hoped ours would too. I love that it looks small from the road, and yet it contains two good-sized bedrooms with their own full bathrooms, two computer work areas, a woodworking shop, a studio of large sculptures, a good-sized kitchen, a dining room for six, a tiny sitting area, a small music area with daybed, and bookshelves, bookshelves, bookshelves. It's a modest house that pleasantly surprises people when they see what a fifteen-hundred-square-foot house can contain, supplying, as it does, all the needs for our work and recreation. Vinyl siding may not be everyone's choice—it wasn't ours, but it was there when we bought the house—but we balance its artificiality with rough cedar

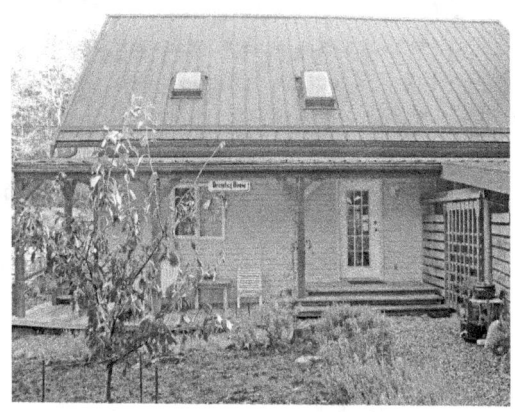

The Wakan's cottage on Gabriola
Island, British Columbia, Canada

posts and decking. Along with a metal roof, you would think our
house is a mishmash, but it all works, topped off with five skylights
that shine like little eyes in the night, allowing the surrounding
trees to come inside the house and also releasing the interior to the
sky. In addition, our little cottage looks out on our orchards, where
we have labored for the past twenty years, and it also stores the
product of our labors in its cupboards.

Our small house allows us our authentic selves. Even the fact
that we didn't build it ourselves, but bought it from folks who
had built it and lived in it, reminds us constantly that where we
settle is merely a caravanserai, a place of comings and goings.

Perhaps, whatever the style, if a house or office building
truly represents the occupants and isn't some keeping-up-
with-the-next-door-neighbors, wowing-the-world kind of
structure, it is a happy building. Wouldn't you think that an
architect would want to build a happy building, a structure
that would make their clients content? Not always.

The homes built by Frank Lloyd Wright and Corbusier—
neither of them particularly happy individuals—were notorious
for leaking. "Move the table," was Wright's advice to a client
who complained that the roof was leaking onto his dining
table. And in 1935, a client, Madame Savoye, wrote to Corbusier
about the famous house they had commissioned: "It is raining
in the hall, it's raining on the ramp and the wall of the garage is
absolutely soaked. . . . it's still raining in my bathroom, which

floods in bad weather, as the water comes in through the skylight. The gardener's walls are also wet through." Eventually, the Savoyes deserted their avant-garde house.

The workers who it was planned would occupy houses built by Le Corbusier in Pessac, France, refused to live in them because they were too far from their workplace, possibly the first consideration for workers' homes. Corbusier viewed a house as a "machine for living." Eventually, Corbusier was forced to admit that "You know, it is life that is right and the architect who is wrong." People didn't want to live in severe boxes, no matter how functional they were, and one can see other groups of houses designed by Corbusier for the working class that later had their exposed terraces roofed and their open spaces divided. Those workers' buildings were solid, though, one cannot deny that.

Then there is Frank Gehry, who appears to be able to crush a sheet of paper and construct a building in the exact shape of the crumpled paper, or who takes a cube and cuts a corner off to insert another cube and so builds up his sculptural structures as happily as artists who are allowed to freely express themselves. Gehry's buildings enrapture, but do they function?

Certainly, looking at Foundation Louis Vuitton, the Wiseman Art Museum, the Dancing House, the Guggenheim in Bilbao, the DZ Bank building, and the Walt Disney Concert hall, one can only assume Gehry crumpled loads of paper and had enormous fun in the process. Whether these sensational buildings are able to fulfill their interior functional needs, however, may be questioned. Did Gehry make his clients happy? Are the people who use the buildings and attend the functions in them uplifted by what they see? I remember visiting the Guggenheim in New York; I was impressed with Frank Lloyd Wright's design—sensational for its time—but viewing art while climbing a ramp is not my idea of optimal viewing. The building very much upstaged its function.

Of course, the Bilbao residents were delighted as literally millions flocked to their depressed town to view Gehry's Guggenheim Museum there. The building paid for itself in three years with the folks swarming the town, and the "Bilbao Effect" was sought by many other depressed towns. So, I suppose it did bring happiness to some. But, as someone asked, "Was the Bilbao Guggenheim built to spread culture or to spread money?"

I may have drifted a little away from my topic of happy architecture, but now I'm back with a list of buildings that made me smile—perhaps made me completely happy—when I viewed them. They include Moshe Safdie's Habitat 67 in Montreal that I, among thousands, lined up to view. And it was well worth seeing, but in time, the concrete leaked, the building's air ducts molded, and the moderate cost of the units swelled to over a million dollars each. Oh dear! Does happiness always have a price?

The stave church in Bergen, Norway, was more to my taste. This small church, despite being a reconstruction, filled me with an awe that the Hagia Sophia and the large cathedrals never did. The dragon carvings adorning the roof reminded me that behind Christianity were generations of other, perhaps more simple, ways of worshiping the unknown.

The Royal Crescent in Bath, England, made me enormously happy when I saw it. I was amused to find that, although all the fronts of the houses are identical, thus setting up the wonderful rhythm of the crescent, the backs were left to the individual owners' devices and are a jumble of differing doors, roofs, and windows—"Queen Anne fronts and Mary Anne backs," as it has been described.

Perhaps the building that made me most happy on my travels was Jim Thompson's house in Bangkok, for it was recycled from six antique Thai houses, and as must be known by now, I am a big fan of recycling. Jim Thompson centered his revival of the Thai silk trade on this complex house, which was both his home and amazing shop, filled with luscious silks from floor to ceiling. He went on holiday in the highlands one day and never returned. The mystery of his death—was it tigers or sabotage?—still remains. Jim Thompson, before the war, was actually a practicing architect, so he can be listed as someone who is able to make a happy building.

Happy architecture cannot guarantee happiness. Happy architecture cannot prevent sadness. But it can contribute to contentment.

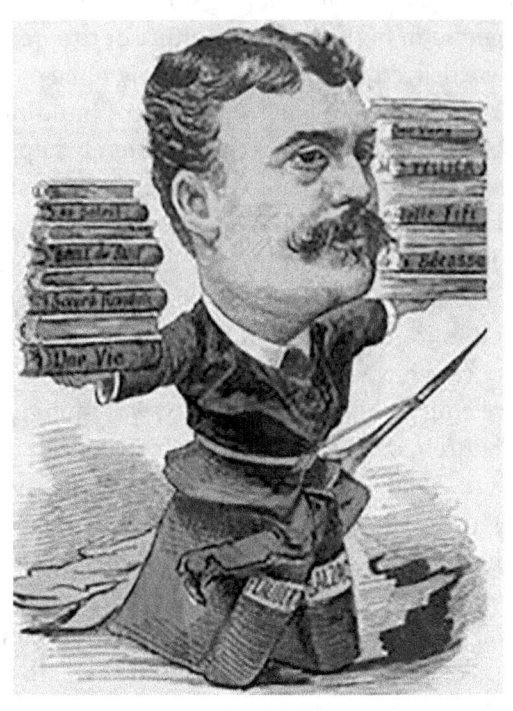

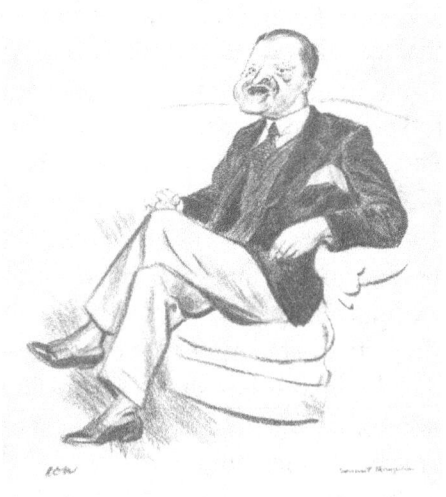

Caricatures of [top] Guy de Maupassant and [bottom] W. Somerset Maugham

the art of
short-story writing

I HAVE BEEN THINKING LATELY THAT I SHOULD TRY
writing some short stories before I kick the bucket. Of course,
I have told stories in my personal essays, but they were, for the
most part, true stories. I know there is an art to short-story
writing, an art I am unfamiliar with. Such ignorance has never
inhibited me in the past when I have lent my hand to pottery,
painting, sculpture, embroidery, and quilting, without any
teacher in sight.

You would think that, being Canadian, I would turn to
Alice Munro as a model, but no. Her coming-of-age, small-
town-Ontario-girl pieces do not really resonate with me,
although I am a small-town girl, but for some reason, I never
really came of age. Also, I have never laughed out loud from
reading Munro's oeuvres, an odd requirement, perhaps, but
one I demand from a full-living author. I do hope people laugh
out loud occasionally when they read my writing because
laughing is such a good, disarming movement of the muscles.

Still, considering Canadian influences, although I've been
reveling in the short stories of Margaret Atwood ("Stone
Mattress") and Zsuzsi Gartner ("Better Living Through Plastic
Explosives") and wishing I had their acerbic wit and brilliant
imaginations, it wouldn't be those authors I would turn to for
guidance either.

Instead, I would turn to someone enormously popular
in his time, though rarely read today, Somerset Maugham. I
would also look for guidance to Maugham's own role model

for short stories, Guy de Maupassant, the French writer. De Maupassant had actually been a guest at Maugham's mother's salons. Their writings on Malay rubber plantations (Maugham) and endless adultery (de Maupassant) are a bit alien to me, and yet . . . and yet . . . it is to these two I will turn for some guidelines that I might follow for writing short stories, until I follow my own. I think the reason I chose these role models was because I read them avidly in my teens; what we do in our teens sticks with us into our dotage.

At the end of the Second World War, European culture suddenly flooded starved Britain. I wallowed in French movies such as *Les Enfants du Paradis* and *The Well-Digger's Daughter*, *Quai des Orfèvres* and *Beauty and the Beast*. Their startling sensuality awakened something in my adolescent self. Our household was an inhibited one, and this French invasion bowled me over. Along with it came the above mentioned writer, Guy de Maupassant, whose stories I read greedily, seeking a role model for what a woman might be. Hardly suitable role-model reading, but what did I know at that age? I certainly had no model in my mother, a woman who never even began to fulfill her potential until it was too late. I noted that Maugham had also read all of de Maupassant before he was eighteen.

Remembering those years and stuck in my present aspiration to be a short-story writer, I got de Maupassant's complete short stories from the library. Well, actually, our system didn't have a copy, so I had to go to Interlibrary Loan for one. Even the fame of someone such as de Maupassant, who, as father of the short-story form, influenced so many other notable short-story writers, fades over the centuries.

And what has reading those thousand pages taught me about short-story writing? Well, mostly, that they must tell a good tale. Most of de Maupassant's stories are in the format of the writer meeting someone at a dinner or in a bar who relates a story. This tale needs a setting, then a beginning, a climax, and a surprising ending. In this last respect, I reckoned, de Maupassant only muffed a few.

Within this telling, de Maupassant still had time to discuss more general matters, such as the futility of war, nature versus nurture, our eternal aloneness, and the pondering over many things on which we never think when we are young. While de Maupassant's generalizations about women would jar today's readers, some of his ideas strike me as very current, such as: "A place of worship represents the homage paid by man to the 'Unknown.' The more extended our thoughts and our views become, the more the Unknown diminishes, and the more places of worship will decay."

But more than de Maupassant's content, I enjoy his strongly shaped stories, efficiently told, with a rabbit's kick in the end. I call it that because it is the surprise kick a rabbit gives when it is being chased before it finally disappears. De Maupassant's story "Boule de Suif" has such an ending, as has Maugham's best-known story, "Rain." I suppose, it is really called a denouement. In both stories, it consists of just a few well-chosen words. When it comes to rabbits' kicks, Maugham also didn't like "ends that are left lying about, themes that are propounded and not resolved, and a climax that is foreseen and then eluded." He added, "The end should be unexpected but when the story is reread the reader will see that it is inevitable."

Having ploughed through a thousand pages of adultery, I have now definitively selected de Maupassant as my role model for future short-story writing efforts, and I have three hundred of his stories to learn from. By the way, Guy de Maupassant penned his own epitaph: "I have coveted everything and taken pleasure in nothing." I won't follow him in this respect, and I hope mine can read: "I have taken pleasure in everything and coveted nothing."

I am not given to reading bestsellers or the Book of the Month. "The oldest books are still only just out to those who have not read them." So said Samuel Butler, and I am in entire agreement. My reading tends to meander according to my interests of the moment. I might very well be reading a book on Istanbul museums and find a mention of an unknown author that intrigues me. I immediately order their books from the library, and each one has links that I am free to follow up on. Many of the links lead back to authors who were once well known but now can rarely be found on the shelves of small libraries—authors such as de Maupassant and the writers who idolized him, such as O. Henry and the already mentioned Somerset Maugham.

I came to Maugham again recently via the curious subject of children sent to Canada from Dr. Barnardo's orphanages in England. One of the doctor's daughters, Syrie, became Maugham's wife. His name jogged memories of those teen years when I read everything by him I could lay hands on. Now, curious about the possibility that I might try writing short fiction myself, I recalled his strength in this genre and ordered books on the topic, as well as buying a second-hand copy of his complete short stories.

Ostensibly, we seem to have nothing in common. He was a doctor, a spy, gay, a man who traveled and stayed extensively in the colonial East (I lived two years in Japan, but that is not quite the same). He was said to be sophisticated, a misogynist, malicious, and racist. None of which can be used to describe me, at least I hope not. However, I do feel so akin to him and feel he could guide me on my way toward the understanding of the art of short-fiction writing. So what do we have in common?

First, Maugham and I are both observers from a place well outside the passing scene, dispassionate or, in my case, maybe a slightly passionate observer. Maugham was an outsider because he was born in the British Embassy in Paris and felt more at home in France than in England. He lived abroad most of his life. I, as a twin (one in one hundred at that time), a grandchild of Jewish immigrants living in a WASP area during my childhood, and an immigrant to Canada for most of my life, can feel a twinge of similarity in our backgrounds as outsiders that put us in good observer status. We both had speech defects as children. Maugham stammered, as did I, and I also could never pronounce my 'r's, which was unfortunate, as my twin's name was Ruth Rudd. Of his stammer, Maugham wrote, "What has influenced my life more than any other single thing has been my stammer. Had I not stammered I would probably have gone to Cambridge as my brothers did, perhaps have become a don and every now and then published a dreary book about French literature."

Maugham's teller in his short stories, his lead character, is almost always himself and, as a personal essayist, that might well be my approach if I ever get started. He denied he was the storyteller, however, and said it was just a device "that made it possible for the writer to tell no more than he knows. Making no claim to omniscience, he can frankly say when a motive or occurrence is unknown to him, and thus often give his story a plausibility that it might otherwise lack." Maugham added, "If the author can in no way keep himself out of his work it might be better if he put in as much of himself as possible." On this point Maugham mentioned the danger that the author might put in too much of himself and thus be as boring "as a talker who insists on monopolizing the conversation."

Maugham tells his stories straight—no elaborate backgrounds or scenery descriptions are provided. The reader continually knows exactly who is doing what to whom. This is a condition I ask from my poetry and so I may well demand it of my short-story writing too. Many of his stories were told to him or were from his personal experience (lightly disguised), and the few stories I have told in my essays came from my life as a social work student in the slums of Birmingham, my years as a mother and housewife, or my travels, particularly my years in Japan. Nicholas Shakespeare, the British novelist, writes of Maugham's stories, "Only a trembling leaf separates hope from despair. Suffering doesn't ennoble. The murderer doesn't get caught. The wages of sin aren't always death. Men hate those they have injured. Beneath the mousiest woman lurks the most vicious Valkyrie." I could well write stories along these lines myself.

So Maugham's world-weary style suits my cynical, agnostic questioning of what I see as a vaguely crazy world, if I am to choose a role model for writing my stories. Of religion, Maugham's quote, "What mean and cruel things men can do for the love of God," echoes my own feelings. Britannica says of Maugham, "Maugham explains his philosophy of life as a resigned atheism and a certain skepticism about the extent of man's innate goodness and intelligence; it is this that gives his work its astringent cynicism." Ah! "Astringent cynicism"—now that's what I'd like critics to notice about my writing. On being cynical, Maugham has one of his characters say: ". . . if to look truth in the face and not resent it when it's unpalatable. And take human nature as you find it, smiling when it's absurd and grieved without exaggeration when it's pitiful is to be a cynic, then I suppose I'm a cynic."

Maugham said, "Tolerance is indifference;" and the experience of living on an island where people are very forgiving and I am not, has me nodding in agreement with Maugham. The following quotes also reverberate: "People ask for criticism when they only want praise"; "Writing is the supreme solace"; "It's very hard to be a gentleman and a writer"; "When I read a book I seem to read it with my eyes only, but now and then I come across a passage, perhaps only a phrase, which has a meaning for me, and it becomes part of me."

Maugham took his characters from life and from stories he was told. For example, he took the two lead people in his famous story "Rain," the prostitute and the missionary, from passengers on a ship he took from Honolulu to Pago Pago. About the living model, he said, "You are much more likely to depict a character who is a recognizable human being with his own individuality if you have a living model." Yes, I will do the same, but try to disguise them better than Maugham did when, for example, in "Cakes and Ale," he pinned Thomas Hardy down.

Other bits of advice from Maugham that I shall definitely consider are:

"Leave out everything that doesn't serve the dramatic value."

"A story should have a beginning, a middle, and an end."

"Then I discovered it was because I spoke the truth. It was so unusual that people thought it humorous."

Regarding his spy, Ashenden, "People sometimes thought him heartless because he was more often interested in others than attached to them."

"When he [an author] succeeds, he has forced you for a time to accept his view of the universe and has given you the pleasure of following out the pattern he has drawn on the surface of chaos. But he seeks to prove nothing. He paints a picture and sets it before you. You can take it or leave it."

Maugham's definition of a short story: "A piece of fiction that has unity of impression and that can be read at a single sitting." Later, he added, "It must sparkle, excite or impress."

"When idealism and realism clash, idealism must give way."

"The short story does not aim at the development of character nor does it aim at the discovery of character."

"The short story should occupy itself with one moment in time."

He had a clinical detachment (more interested than attached) and was ever the observer, seeing humanity's strengths and weaknesses.

Maugham liked rogues and scoundrels more than good people.

Yes, I know his stories are dated but then, so am I. After all this, and after reading Maugham's complete short stories for the umpteenth time (and not forgetting that I recently read a thousand pages of de Maupassant for the second time), I may well be ready to set pen to paper and surprise myself.

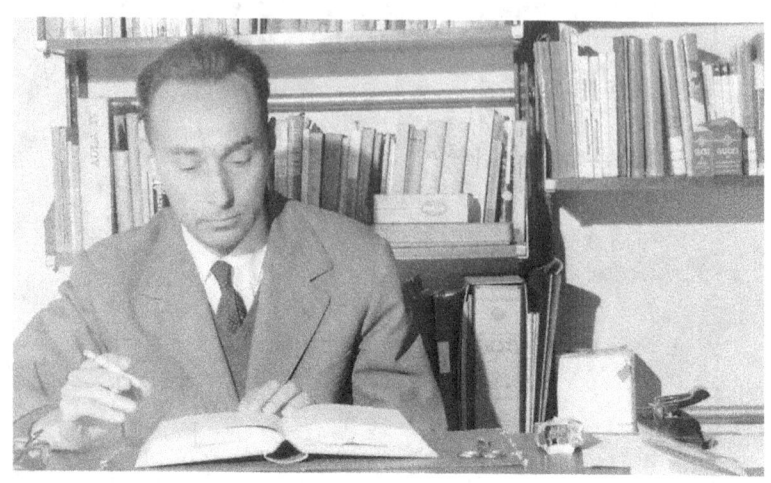

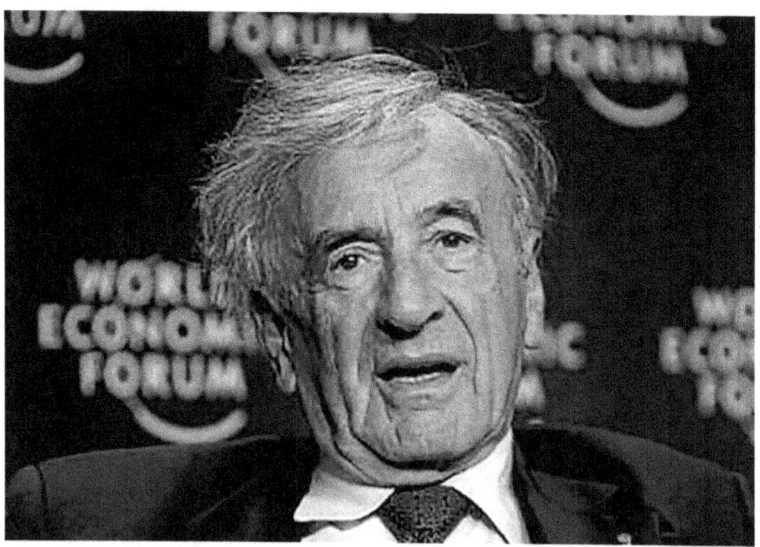

[top] Chemist and writer, Primo Levi and [bottom] writer and
activist Elie Wiesel, both survivors of the Holocaust

the art of
survival

A NEIGHBOR DIED RECENTLY. HE WAS A PLEASANT MAN, suffering as an alcoholic. His children staged a garage sale, and among his modest five books on sale was a copy of *The Truce* by Primo Levi. I have no idea why Primo Levi was of interest to this man. My neighbor was not Jewish, nor a survivor or relative of a survivor of the camps, nor a chemist, nor interested in science, as far as I knew. Yet here was a Primo Levi I hadn't read sitting in its nice case at my deceased neighbor's garage sale. "How well can one ever know another person?" I asked myself.

If anyone was a survivor, Primo Levi was, but he also carried the guilt of survivors. Levi was a chemist, which allowed him to work in a plant making synthetic rubber instead of experiencing the killing conditions of the outside laborers. His book *The Truce*, the story of his journey home from the camp, is another story of his survival skills. His need to survive was his need to tell, to make people understand what had gone on in the camps, to bear witness. Even in the camps, to make oneself understood was an important survival skill.

Levi had to work on survival skills as a child because he was small and Jewish, and was bullied at school. Along with his training as a hiker and skier, he had both the physical ability and the psychological strength of a survivor. The people who survived the camps often married and had children, as if to replace all those lost. Primo Levi did likewise.

His death was believed to be a suicide caused by depression. It is true he had bouts of depression, but there was no physical evidence that he killed himself—no witnesses, no note. Surely, a chemist can find more certain ways of killing oneself than falling down a narrow stairwell. It is recorded that he went out to look for the concierge and told his mother's nurse to listen for the telephone, hardly the words of someone about to kill himself. Probably, the side effects of the medicine he was taking for depression caused him to tip forward over the low banister rail and tumble down. An unlikely suicide candidate, he had said about life in the camps, "One is too busy trying to survive there to have energy left to think about anything else, even suicide." After the camps, he was surely too busy bearing witness.

How does one survive very difficult times? Is there an art to surviving that can be learned? Surviving doesn't just mean staying alive or getting by; a certain thriving is implied. The first thing, I think, is to see clearly the difficult situation one is in—anything from being trapped in an unhealthy marriage, to being unable to find the next mortgage payment, to having to live among "the enemy"—maybe in hiding, maybe as a persecuted minority group.

The next thing, I think, is to make up one's mind not to be a victim in the situation. I think, for myself, in the "no exit" situations I have experienced in my life, the problem has often been how to stay a mensch, a full human being, a being with integrity and honor.

Yes, how to survive means more than just skill at hiding, finding food and shelter, and avoiding the enemy. Surviving means not just being human, but being a better human. In this fast-changing world, it is so hard to keep up. Many times, I feel so distant from all that is going on that I just want to roll over and sleep forever. But that is me in my most negative state. The other me wants to learn a few new skills so I at least know what is being talked about and so that, even if I can't keep up, at least I don't isolate myself through laziness. So, survival depends on adaptation, on change, and these days, that means changing fast.

Mindstate is such a big factor in survival. Successful survival can begin with just small steps. Let's take the difficult, but not very threatening, situation of becoming old. I am aging and no longer have as much energy as I had even ten years ago. My to-do list, as a householder and a writer, used to stretch to two pages. These days, such overwhelming lists throw me into depression, so I start each day by listing only three or four things to do that day. I begin with the one that needs the most energy and intelligence and get that done first thing in the morning. By taking just this one small step, my life is not only bearable, but even exhilarating, as each small task is accomplished in its correct time. This first step not only overcomes my despair, but also builds up my stamina. We are not speaking of Auschwitz here, we are speaking of an average human being who needs to give their life some meaning beyond the daily grind, the need to survive creatively with an aging mind and body.

Yes, intelligence and quick wit often help us adapt, but better yet is to have a well-developed imagination. We need an imagination, not to take us into the escapism of an unreal world, but an imagination to help find creative ways of dealing with the insufferable problems of the world we are in. Trying is better than giving up. When no solution is forthcoming, I've found cleaning and weeding help. When I'm doing such routine jobs, small ways of facing problems, or even avoiding them, often surface. If I concentrate on my body, my mind is left to its own devices to find a creative way out of the no-exit situations I sometimes find myself in. Now, I'm not saying that such steps would have helped in the death camps. I remember a doctor friend who helped camp survivors. He gave much thought as to what allowed a person to survive healthily and what caused a person to be defeated readily in such terrible conditions. I don't think he ever was able to come up with any solid conclusions.

It is important, however, not to compare one's situation to unspeakable tragedies, for we all suffer in different ways. Sometimes we can stumble and fall because of a small stone; sometimes we can survive an avalanche without turning a hair.

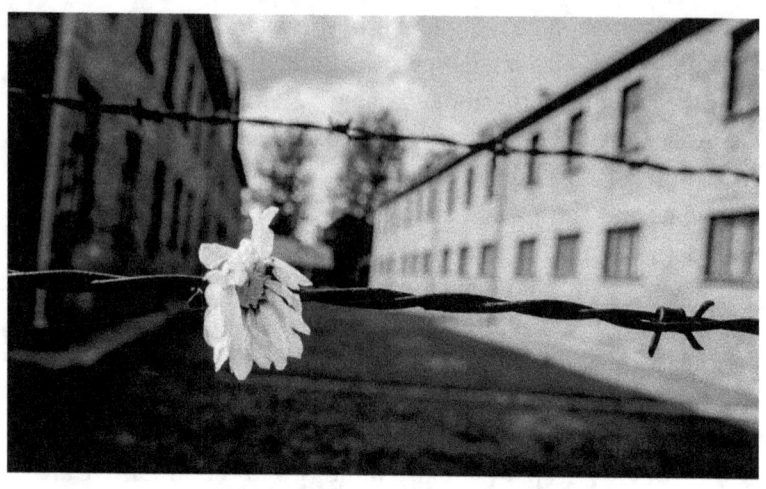

Petar Milošević, Sight at Auschwitz concentration camp, 2012.

Fear petrifies, and survival calls for action, or at least conscious inaction. With fear, one is unable to think clearly and rationally; yet, in disaster situations, we need to. You can't believe that whatever is happening to you is happening to you, and that halts your processing it. One cannot prepare in advance for every contingency life throws our way. One can't always be on red alert; that is no way to live. Surviving doesn't need heroic measures; it does, however, demand a certain preparation early in life, not for particular emergencies, but to establish a general "wish to live" attitude.

How to sit out the storm, or whether to confront it— that is the real problem. And if one chooses to confront it, the question then is how to gather one's intelligence, imagination, and physical stamina to come up with a survival solution.

Once, I was giving a memoir-writing workshop and, wanting to finish on a positive note, I had the attendees draw up a kind of life-ledger, putting all the good events of their lives in one column and all the bad times in another. I asked them to be sure to provide one more good time than bad time. As they were doing the exercise, I did it along with them, and the startling revelation came to me that all the good times

I'd noted down didn't seem quite so good now, and from all the bad times I seemed to have emerged a more interesting person. The good and the bad seemed to have almost switched places, or at least have intermingled. Life is a bittersweet thing, and we can't avoid all the pain it will bring us, nor cling to the pleasure, for it too will pass. As my daughter advised me before I went into hospital to have a breast removed, "It all depends on your attitude."

One needs a reason to survive and mine is curiosity, the curiosity of a child wanting to know how the story will end. Can curiosity possibly be my survival tool? It would be so convenient if it was.

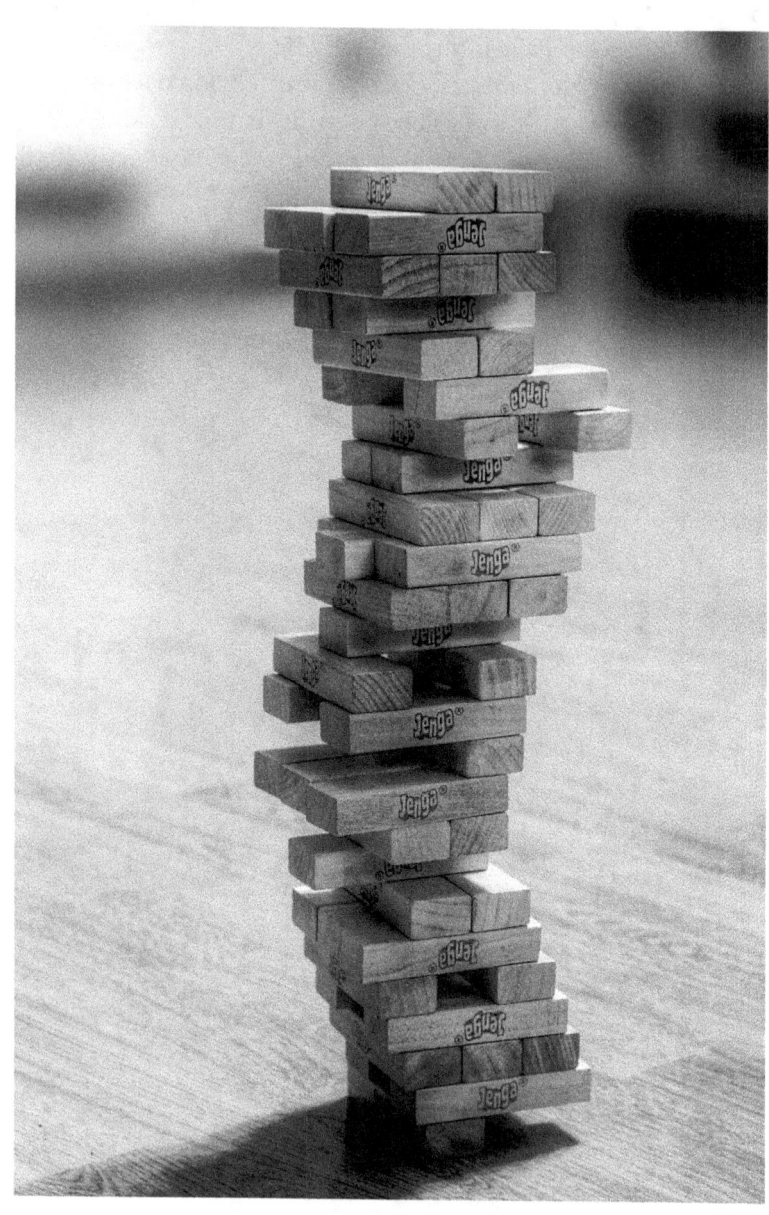

Jenga tower balanced on one block

the art of
unblocking

WHEN IT CAME TO DECIDING WHAT ART FORM I WOULD discuss in the last chapter of this book, I was flooded with ideas. I started three or four essays boldly and then petered out on each of them. It occurred to me that I had momentary writer's block, not from lack of ideas, as is usually the case, but from a congestion of too many. I remembered I had dwelt on writer's block a little at the beginning of this book, and as it now occupied my mind, I decided I would make bookends of the topic and finish by considering the art of *un*blocking. Block dissolved!

Although I have dilettanted through many of the arts in my lifetime and in this book, the only art form I have come anywhere near perfecting is the art of helping others unblock. In the many workshops I have given, whether by using encouraging words, a pat on the back, a push from behind, or a kick in the bottom, I have played a small part in helping a few artists and writers overcome their blocks and open to their unique talents.

As you probably know by now, I like summarizing things, so here, to clarify ways of unblocking the creative drive, both for myself and for you, I will consider them point by point. Some will negate others, but that is the way when we are all individuals and need our own particular way of unblocking that suits best where we are at the moment.

- Get re-inspired by watching people who have worked hard in their field, maybe one not connected to yours. When I get stuck, I watch professional ice-skating and wonder at the miracle that I am seeing while not forgetting the hours of work the person must have put in to reach that stage.

- Put your project aside until the urge to create returns. Just go away and play. Get out that child's package of crayons and scribble.

- Often a block is caused by a momentary drop in self-worth. So low self-esteem, from whatever cause, may need to be looked at, rather than focusing on the present piece of creativity that seems to be causing trouble. Our inner critic can cause this problem, but whose negating voice is it really, this voice that accentuates the negatives of our creativity rather than the positives? It says, "This is garbage!" "How can you be so stupid?" "You'll never amount to much! "What will people think?" "You're doing it the wrong way." Well, I'm sure you could add a load more. It's the inner voice that needs blocking, needs squashing, needs dealing with. You can't create and criticize at the same time.

- When I am doing a cryptic crossword and come to a clue that I think is an anagram, I rearrange the letters of the words that I think might make the required anagram and write them at the edges of a circle. This breaks up the old words and allows me to see new patterns. As a writer, sometimes I use the same technique by rearranging paragraphs to see if I can view the writing from a fresh point of view. Similarly, in painting, photograph a portion of the canvas, blow it up, and play with it. Why not turn the work upside down? That's how Kandinsky came to see, for the first time, how a painting didn't need subject matter. Anything that presents the art in a way that allows you to see it differently, from a new perspective, is good. A new slant may just be the thing that gets you unblocked and going again.

- Try a different medium or genre. If I am stuck in an essay, I try to present the same ideas in blank verse, or might even reduce the whole mess to a rather nice haiku. If you are using oils, try watercolors; if writing a sonata, try writing a song. Write, paint, sculpt, or dance something that makes you feel awkward, embarrassed maybe, or just out of your depths and watch what turns up.

- Simply ask for help. In order to do this, you must be willing to at least listen to criticism without taking it personally. Sometimes just talking about the block may dissolve it as you find yourself presenting solutions which you had never thought of when you were just wailing at the block.

- Diversion, diversion, diversion. There's nothing like it for ignoring the block while you allow your creative self to re-energize. I often choose scrubbing the kitchen floor, which gives shiny results while at the same time keeping me occupied and off the computer. Stop and clean up your studio, study, or workspace. There is nothing like physical labor to keep you in your body and let your busy (or not busy) mind sort itself out.

- Stop anticipating an outcome, even if you have a deadline. Stop the questions: "What will they think?" "Would a publisher even want this?" "How can I make this turn into dollars?" Just play. Is that so hard?

- Take a leap into something you have always been a little afraid of. I am strictly a poet and essayist, so when I feel frustrated, I toy with writing short fiction, something for which I have no skill. If you work on small canvases, stretch a large one and throw yourself at it.

- Sometimes what you have chosen to undertake is so big that it is daunting. Take a deep breath and jump. Believe me, once the first sentence is down, the first brushstroke is on the canvas, the rest will follow.

- Creative confusion—too many choices, as I had when I started this chapter—can be equally as blocking to creativity as no choices; as ideas get in each other's way, your energy gets jammed. Decide on parameters that help you focus on just one of your ideas, and put the others aside to be picked up later or forgotten entirely.

- Blocks can be a sign of depleted energy. When I am in flow, I write, write, write. When the words coming out start to feel wooden, I stop and give myself time to re-energize. Exhaustion and block sometimes seem like the same thing. Consider whether your creative block may actually have a physical cause—lack of sleep, hunger. Check your physical needs and see they are being met.

- Some artists recommend you push through because pain is part of creation, making a creative act sound a little like giving birth to a child, which I suppose it is. They say there is no point in waiting for inspiration; if you keep plodding on, the muse will arrive in the end. Picasso said, "Inspiration exists, but it has to find us working." Go to the studio/writing desk/piano each day and put in your time. Don't wait for inspiration. Put in those 10,000 hours to get to Carnegie Hall. Others say nothing good can come of "pushing through." Still, it just may work for you.

- My personal solution for blocks is to have a number of projects going at one time, so that if one isn't working, I can ignore it and see if another will set me in flow.

- If you are starting to think negatively of the work that is not going the way you want it to, try and look on it more kindly. Saying it is "crap" or "stupid" is not going to help. As David Bellos wrote, "Optimism alone allows you to do something new."

- Finally, in all cases, honor the pause. It may not seem fruitful, but allow it to be. Don't be impatient and demanding. If you can't meet the deadline, you can't. It won't be the end of the world.

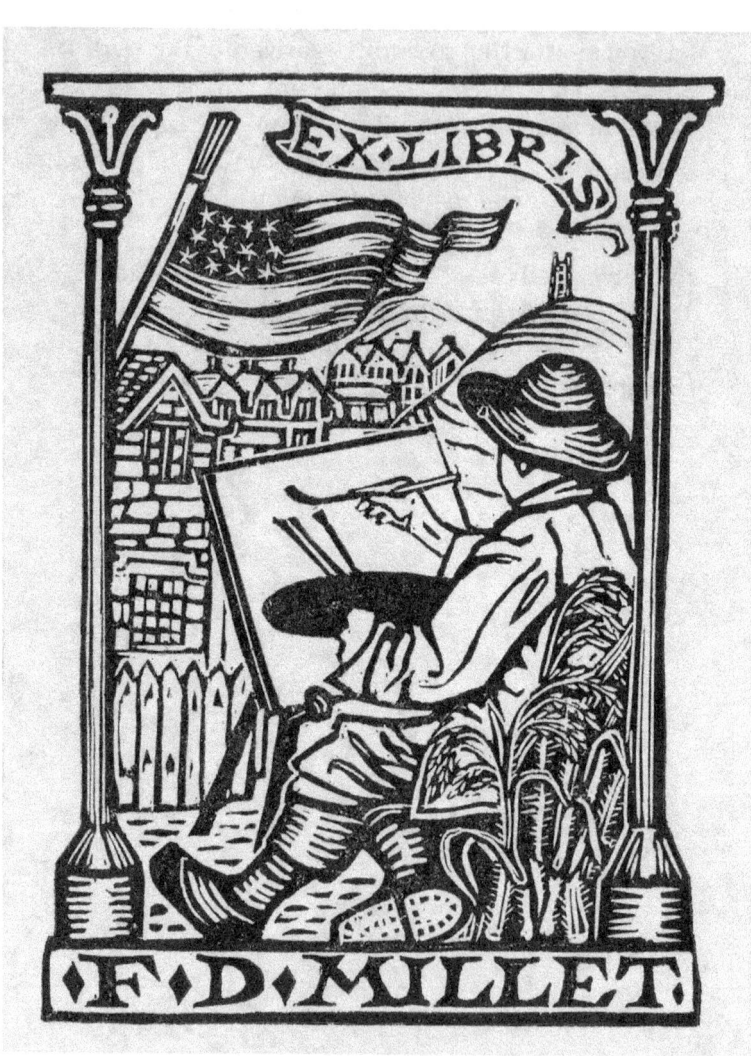

Bookplate of American painter Francis Davis Millet

afterword

I STARTED THIS VENTURE BY WRITING ABOUT ART AND how our viewing of the term has evolved to include crafts, and extended from there to encompass a range of human behavior that involves the intense use of the imagination along with the acquiring of technical skills. Art, I concluded, was anything done with focus and skill. The abilities needed for the practice of "the arts," in particular, under my magnifying glass, seemed to morph into listing the abilities we need in order to practice anything in life.

The "arts" I have considered in this book have all, at various times, absorbed my consciousness, and even though I have skimmed through most of them, I still have enough experience of them and skill in presenting them, I hope, to entice you into exploring some of them.

Human behavior does not, on the whole, interest me. There are only so many plots, and most of them are repetitive and boring. What does hold me, however, are the rare moments of "Aha!" when someone has put two ideas together that have never been put together before (at least not by them). Those epiphany moments—whether as small as juxtaposing a few well-chosen words or as large as to cause great shifts in our perception of life—are the times when I cry out loud in admiration of the act and encourage the creative endeavor. As my husband so wisely said, "A creative life is itself a creation."

notes

18 I would like to attach this note, for what it's worth, to the
mention of Emin's unmade bed. One morning, my husband
called me into our bedroom to see the morning light on our
rumpled sheets. The pattern was of heaving dunes in some
far-off land and was totally enchanting.

48 *Rikka* done today can be so large and striking that often a couple
of practitioners will spend a whole day on an arrangement,
which demands a lot of physical strength to complete.

55 Buson's illustrations for Bashō's book, *Narrow Road to the Deep
North*, are the best known haiga in the classical style. For
a viewing of a current master in the more traditional style
using a brush, not a camera, check out Kuniharu Shimizu.
Another of today's more traditional haiga artist, this time
non-Japanese,is Ion Codrescu. Jim Kacian, the expert on all
things haiku, has a great essay linking haiga to comic book
art. A few worthwhile websites to visit are <simplyhaiku.com>,
<haikupoetshut.com>, and <gendaihaiku.com>. For a daily
dose of haiga, visit <dailyhaiga.org>.

109 YouTube has a wonderful video on which you can hear Ms.
DiDonato explaining and singing examples of bel canto.

124 John Ruskin's work is in the public domain. This piece
appeared in *Modern Painters* in 1843.

129 Michael Dylan Welch's piece was first published in *Quill and
Parchment*, January 2012. It is used here with his permission.

159 Three copious books on the subject of Outsider Art are
Outsider Art by Jean-Louis Ferrier; *Vernacular Visionaries:
International Outsider Art*, edited by Annie Carlano; and the
very academic *Outsider Art*, edited by Zolberg and Cherbo.
William Swislow's blog, <www.interestingideas.com>, covers
a range of outsiders' art.

164 Darger's life and work can seen in Jessica Yu's documentary, *In the Realms of the Unreal,* available on YouTube.

images

6   Wassily Kandinsky, *Free Curve to the Point - Accompanying Sound of Geometric Curves*, 1925. Ink on paper. 15.7 x 11.8 inches (40.0 x 30.2 cm). Metropolitan Museum of Art, New York City. WC PD

10   Elias Wakan, [top] *Landscape 4*; [bottom] *Fold 4*. Images used with permission of the artist.

14   [top] Sculpture by Andy Goldsworthy in the Royal Botanic Garden Edinburgh. Photograph by Karora, 2007. WC PD [bottom] Andy Warhol's *Campbell Soup Cans* in the Museum of Modern Art, New York City, 2008. Photograph by Group de Besanez. WC CC

19   Damien Hirst, *Hymn*, 1999–2005. Painted bronze. 19.5 x 10.9 x 6.7 feet (595.3 x 334.0 x 205.7 cm). Photograph by Chaeyoung907, 2019. WC CC

23   Banksy, *The Kissing Coppers*. Stencil Graffiti. First seen in 2005 at the Prince Albert Pub in Brighton, England. After being vandalized, it was removed and sold in 2014 at a U.S. auction to a private buyer for $575,000. The sale caused much backlash, much of it accusing the pub of making a mockery of street art by selling and privatizing the piece. Photograph by ShoZu, 2005. WC CC

26   Elias Wakan, [top] *Sliced Ice*; [bottom] *Segue*. Images used with permission of the artist.

38   Evacuees of Japanese ancestry at work on art projects at relocation center during World War II. U.S. National Archives and Records Administration, College Park, Maryland. WC PD [top left] Poston Relocation Center, Poston, Arizona. Mr. Hitomi carving a bird from wood. Photographer unknown, 1945. [top right] Jerome Relocation Center, Denson, Arkansas. A woman prepares a wall plaque

of artificial flowers made from tissue paper. Photograph by Tom Parker, 1943. [bottom left] Manzanar Relocation Center, Manzanar, California. Students in art class. Photograph by Dorothea Lange, 1942. [bottom right] Manzanar Relocation Center, Manzanar, California. Women making artificial flowers. Photograph by Dorothea Lange, 1942.

44 *Ikebana* by Henry Kellner. Photographed by Henry Kellner, 2017. WC CC

46 Calligraphy by Sonja Arntzen; used with her permission.

49 Elias Wakan, *Field of Dreams*. Used with permission of the artist.

52 Haiga by Carole MacRury; used with her permission.

55 [top] Haiga by Matsuo Bashō (1644–94). [bottom] Haiga by Carole MacRury; used with her permission.

56 Haiga by Jim Swift; used with his permission.

58 Julia Child's kitchen at the National Museum of American History (Smithsonian Institution). Photograph by Kevin Burkett, 2012. WC CC

65 Images used with permission of the artist.

68 Dorothea Lange, *Migrant Family*, 1936. Library of Congress's Prints and Photographs division. WC PD

77 Image used with permission of the artist.

78 [top] *Skating in Holland*, c. 1900. Oil on canvas. 12.5 x 18.2 inches (31.8 x 46.4 cm). Attributed to Johan Bartold Jongkind but believed to be a forgery. National Gallery, London. WC PD [bottom] *Portrait of a Young Man*. Egg tempera on wood. Attributed to fifteenth-century painter Piero Pollaiuolo, but believed to be a forgery made in the nineteenth century. WC PD

86 Carl Vilhelm Holsoe, *Woman Reading in an Interior*, early nineteenth century. Oil on canvas. WC PD

91 Image used with permission of the artist.

94 Jean-Honoré Fragonard, *A Young Girl Reading*, c. 1770. Oil on canvas. 31.9 x 25.5 inches (81.1 cm x 64.8). National Gallery of Art, Washington, D.C. WC PD

96 A page of the famous *L'exemplaire de Bordeaux*, a copy of the second edition of the *Essais* with Montaigne's corrections, annotations, and additions for the third (final) edition. This page is from *Essai no. 27* of the first book, entitled "De l'amitié" ("On friendship").

104 Two scenes from *Norma*, by Vincenzo Bellini, performed by the Serbian National Theatre, 2006. Photograph by Miomir Polzović. WC CC

107 Joan Sutherland and Luciano Pavarotti in *I Puritani*, 1976, Photograph by AP Wirephoto. WC PD

108 Maria Callas as Giulia in the opera *La Vestale* by Gaspare Spontini, 1954. Photograph by Teatro alla Scala. WC CC

110 Peter Ilsted, *Interior with Girl Reading*, 1910. WC PD

116 John Singer Sargent, *Spanish Dancer*, 1880. WC PD

119 Image used with permission of the artist.

124 J. M. W. Turner, *Slavers Throwing Overboard the Dead and Dying*, 1840. Oil on canvas. 35.7 x 48.2 inches (90.8 x 122.6 cm). Museum of Fine Arts, Boston. WC PD

127 Alice Rich, *Dissolve*. Used with permission of the artist.

129 Vincent van Gogh, *Bedroom in Arles*, 1888. Oil on canvas. 22.2 x 29.1 inches (56.5 x 74.0 cm). Musée d'Orsay, Paris. WC PD

132 Édouard Manet, *Laundry*, 1875. Oil on canvas. 57.2 x 45.2 inches (145.4 x 114.9 cm). Barnes Foundation, Philadelphia, Pennsylvania. WC PD

135 The Kitchen, House of the Seven Gables, Salem, Massachusetts, c. 1940. Postcard produced by Detroit Publishing Company. New York Public Library, The Miriam and Ira D. Wallach Division of Art, Prints and Photographs. WC PD

138 [top left] Studio publicity portrait of Sterling Hayden for the film *The Asphalt Jungle*, 1950. WC PD [top right] Screenshot of Lana Turner from the trailer for the film *The Postman Always Rings Twice*, 1946. WC PD [bottom] Lauren Bacall and Humphrey Bogart from the film *Dark Passage*, 1947. WC PD

141 from left to right: Richard Long, Edward G. Robinson, Loretta Young, Martha Wentworth, Orson Welles, Philip Merivale, Byron Keith, and unknown actress in *The Stranger*, 1946. WC PD

143 Ann Savage and Tom Neal in *Detour*, 1945. WC PD

144 Calligraphy by Honami Kōetsu and Tawaraya Sôtatsu, seventeenth century. Hanging scroll, ink and gold on paper. 34.5 x 11.1 inches (87.6 x 28.1 cm). Brooklyn Museum. WC PD

146 [left] Calligraphy by Shikō Kataoka of a haiku by Naomi Beth Wakan. [right] Calligraphy by Sonja Arntzen of "Foundation," a poem from the *Kokinshū* anthology. Used with permission.

150 [top] Chixoy, *Furniture as Planters*, 2008. WC PD [bottom] Prakhar Chaudhary, *Throw Them Away or Make Magic*, 2015. WC CC

152 Image used with permission of the artist.

155 Louise Nevelson, *Dawn's Landscape*, 1975. Photograph by smallcurio. WC CC

157 Chris Straw, *Mirror Framed with Antique Rulers*. Used with permission of the artist. In the collection of Alice Rich and Adrian Palmer.

158 Art made by institutionalized patients with schizophrenia. [top] Photograph by cometstarmoon, 2009. WC CC [bottom] Photograph by Thomas.ZAPATA, 2014. WC CC

168 [top] Edward R. Hills House (Hills-DeCaro House), complete remodel designed by Frank Lloyd Wright, 1906. Oak Park, Illinois. Photograph by IvoShandor, 2007. WC CC [bottom] Moshe Safdie, Habitat 67, 1967. Montreal, Canada. Photograph by Rikimedia, 2012. WC CC

171 Image used with permission of the artist.

174 [top] Coll-Toc, Caricature of Guy de Maupassant, 1884. WC PD [bottom] Caricature of W. Somerset Maugham. Artist and date unknown. New York Public Library, Historical and Public Figures Collection. WC PD

182 [top] Primo Levi, 1960. WC PD [bottom] Elie Wiesel speaking at the Annual Meeting of the World Economic Forum in Davos, Switzerland, January 27, 2008. WC CC

186 Petar Milošević, Sight at Auschwitz concentration camp, 2012. WC CC

188 Jenga tower standing on one tile. Photographed by Guma89, 2012. WC CC

194 Francis D. Millet, 1870. Bookplate; woodcut. Library of Congress, Prints and Photographs division. WC PD

WC: Wikimedia Commons
CC: Creative Commons License
PD: Public Domain

about the author

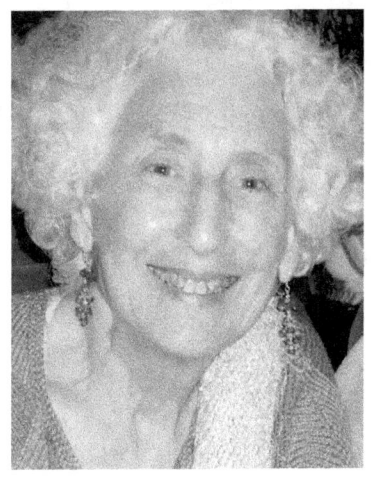

Naomi Beth Wakan, a poet and essayist, has published over fifty books. Her most recent books are the trilogy, *The Way of Haiku, The Way of Tanka*, and *Poetry That Heals* (Shanti Arts). Naomi is a member of The League of Canadian Poets, Haiku Canada, and Tanka Canada. She is the inaugural Poet Laureate of Nanaimo (2013–2016), and has been made the Federation of British Columbia Writers Inaugural Honorary Ambassador. She lives on Gabriola Island with her husband, the sculptor Elias Wakan.

— www.naomiwakan.com